The Stages of Grace

The Stages of Grace

Connie Ruben

Kate O'Neill

Copyright © 2014 by Connie Ruben & Kate O'Neill.

Library of Congress Control Number:		2014912920
ISBN:	Hardcover	978-1-4990-5346-3
	Softcover	978-1-4990-5347-0
	eBook	978-1-4990-5345-6

All rights reserved. No part of this book may be reproduced or transmitted in any form or by any means, electronic or mechanical, including photocopying, recording, or by any information storage and retrieval system, without permission in writing from the copyright owner.

Any people depicted in stock imagery provided by Thinkstock are models, and such images are being used for illustrative purposes only.
Certain stock imagery © Thinkstock.

This book was printed in the United States of America.

Rev. date: 09/15/2014

To order additional copies of this book, contact:
Xlibris LLC
1-888-795-4274
www.Xlibris.com
Orders@Xlibris.com
541382

Contents

Acknowledgement 7

Introduction 9

Chapter One: Grace Finds Me 13

Chapter Two: The Temptation of Hindsight 20

Chapter Three: The Gift of Insight 36

Chapter Four: The Struggle for Adaptability 60

Chapter Five: The Need for Negotiation 82

Chapter Six: The Value of Fallibility 106

Chapter Seven: The Pleasure of Acceptance 124

Chapter Eight: Living in the Present 142

Acknowledgement

I would like to express my gratitude to the many people who saw me through this book—to all those who provided support, talked things over, offered comments, and mostly just put up with me as I kept telling them it was almost done.

I want to send out special thanks to all the caregivers who have not just taken care of Grace but have loved her and have supported me during these last ten years. I owe you all a huge amount of gratitude. I thank Margarita, Korrina, Joyce, Marjorie, Melynne, Maya, and Alvi for being part of my journey. Thanks go out to Regina at Home Instead in Palm Desert and Mark and Joanne at Home Care Assistance in Calgary. You were there for me when I was not sure of the steps to take.

I want to thank Julianne Couch, who was there for me when I was in a panic and ready to stop the writing and start over. Julianne reminded me this was my story and I needed to relax and enjoy the process.

Special thanks to Kate O'Neill, who started off being my ghost writer and ended up being my co-writer. Her dedication to the writing of my story was above and beyond expected. I am honored and humbled to have her in my life.

Special thanks to my dear friend Terri Boyle for taking the picture on the cover of this book. The picture is not necessarily a good picture of either Grace nor I individually, but from the time I saw this picture, I knew this was the perfect symbolization of the love and trust Grace and I share.

I would like to give warm and heartfelt thanks to my husband, Peter, for enabling me to publish this book. Not only was it through Peter that I was blessed to know and love Grace, but the encouragement to do this book and the patience as the editing process began was far more than I could have asked for. Many times, I said it was done, and many times, he encouraged one more read through. His love for his mother is a major part of this book, and I'm forever grateful for the person he is.

Thank you to all in the world that reach outside yourself to care for another. It is not an easy road, and yet it is full of so many blessings.

And lastly, Thank you to Grace. Thank you for accepting me, loving me, trusting me. Thank you for teaching me how to love so unconditionally. Walking through the stages of this disease with you has taught me much about love, patience and acceptance. You have reminded me, through the disease, to take the time to grieve the loss of the person who was there, but then welcome the person who is there now. So much would have been missed in my world if I would have closed my eyes and heart to you once the disease took over. The special memories you have provided will continue throughout my life and I thank you for this. If I could end up being once small piece of the woman you are, even in the depth of this terrible disease, I will be a very happy person. Thank you dear Grace.

Introduction

I rush through the door to the doctor's office, flustered because I am late for this appointment. I look around anxiously for Grace, hoping to find her still in the waiting room, but the receptionist waves me toward one of the smaller offices, explaining that the doctor will be right in. As I step into the room, I see Grace: hands gnarled and bony and folded calmly on her lap, with thin skin that betrays her ninety-three years of age. Her silver hair is neatly styled, framing light blue eyes in a face that has a noble quality, despite the years. She seems quite small in her chair. Her curved back causes her to stoop slightly forward, but when she looks up at me, there is a sense of ease, almost serenity, in her composure. I kneel down beside her to be at eye level. Though I am sure she does not recognize me, there is openness and trust in her eyes. "Do you know who I am?" I ask.

She looks around the room before she answers, "Judging from where we are, I would say that you are the doctor."

"No," I answer evenly. "I'm Connie." Hearing my name, her smile broadens.

She reaches out and holds my hand in both of hers and says with confidence, "Connie, of course you are!"

I have come to be with her for her appointment, but her words, her gesture, and her reassuring smile suddenly rush me into the past. The present melts away and I am once again thirty-two and standing nervously outside a door in the hallway of a building, almost too afraid to knock.

Twenty years ago, I worked for a plastics company in Portland, Oregon, owned by Alberta Mining, a family company headquartered in Calgary, Alberta. The chairman of the company was Bob Ruben, and it was his door that I was standing outside of now. It was business that brought me to Calgary, but it was Peter that brought me to this door. Peter was Bob's son, and we worked together at the plastics company. Knowing I was going to Calgary, Peter had insisted that I stay with his parents even though he was not going to be in town. Somewhat hesitantly, I had accepted, and now, clutching the directions from the airport in my hand, I stood outside the door, worried about what kind of reception I was going to get. Summoning up my courage, I knocked. Soon the door was opened by a lovely woman smoothing her hands over a colorful skirt with a quizzical look on her face.

"You don't know me, but I'm Connie," I said in a rush, anxious to introduce myself. For a brief second, the woman made no response, and I felt a sudden tinge of fear. What if there was some mistake? What if Peter hadn't spoken to his parents?

Then the woman who answered the door smiled a big welcoming smile, took one of my hands in both of hers, and said, "Connie, of course you are! Please come in."

It was a powerful moment for me. Her simple phrase—"of course you are"—made me feel welcome, but more than that, it made me feel like I was exactly the person I was meant to be. Grace's easy words reassured me in a way that I'd never experienced before; in that moment, all things seemed right in the universe. When people talk about love at first sight, they are usually referring to the romantic love of couples, but there are many types of love. Though I did not realize it at that time, I fell in love with Grace instantly. And over the years I learned that it was love well-placed. Grace Ruben is one of those unique people who place others before themselves. I have come to know that this quality is the very essence of Grace. Her kind manner is not a behavior she works to maintain; the naturalness of it cannot be learned or emulated. It is simply who she is. Grace never seeks the limelight and never complains to others. Instead, she offers the world humor and encouragement. Sometimes when people are self-effacing, it stems from a lack of self-worth. Grace, however, has quiet inner strength that comes from contented self-acceptance.

As my thoughts came back to the present, I become aware of myself kneeling beside Grace in the doctor's office. During this transition, however, I am able to hold that first memory of Grace long enough to contrast it with the present moment.

When things change slowly, the extent of the change can go unnoticed. But now I see how much of my mother-in-law and best friend had been stolen by Alzheimer's disease. I realize Grace is gradually fading away. It is painful to see how that vibrant, intelligent woman I first met has become this frail person whose ties to this world are tenuous and fraying.

I look at this woman holding my hand and think about all the stages that she has transitioned through because of her Alzheimer's disease—from a dynamic competent woman, to needing some assistance, to becoming totally dependent, and now to the stage of losing cognizance of her situation and those around her. This last stage is not easy. It is an effort for Grace to make sense of her world. Sometimes panic sets in, and it is difficult to sooth her anxiety. It is challenging to talk with her as she repeats herself and struggles for words. But if I am patient, there are surprising moments when her personality and wit emerge from the fog. These moments remind me that under the shroud of this disease, the same pure, loving soul remains. Some things don't change; some things can't be taken away. My love for Grace is one of them.

I look back at the many stages Grace has transitioned through as a result of this disease, and though I lament her losses along the way, I cherish the fact that I have been with her through it all. I cannot help but reflect on the fact that over this same period, as Grace has grown weaker, I have grown stronger. Much of that I owe to her. She has helped me to feel loved and to feel worthy in ways I thought I would never experience in my life.

This book was written in part to honor Grace Ruben as a profoundly important person, but it was also born of a desire to share with others who have loved ones with Alzheimer's disease what I have experienced as Grace's caregiver and friend. I wanted to capture the emotions, the expected and unexpected issues, the painful times, and the humorous and loving moments that Grace and I have shared as a result of this disease. This is not meant to be a handbook for dealing with Alzheimer's disease, but I hope that by sharing my feelings and experiences, readers may recognize that they are not alone on this particular journey. And so flows this book.

Chapter One

Grace Finds Me

Grace: noun

1. *Elegance or beauty of form, manner, or action.*
2. *A pleasing or attractive quality or endowment.*
3. *Favour or goodwill.*
4. *Mercy, clemency, or pardon.*

I am not a graceful woman. To me, the word *grace* implies insight, a light touch, a kindness that never seems cultivated. True grace flows naturally. From a distance, I might seem calm and poised to some, but in truth, my manner is nothing so impressive. When I am calm, it is because I worked hard to be organized; if I seem poised, it is because I am determined to appear so. When I was young, my family situation required me to be self-reliant; I learned to value strength and control. Those traits empowered me and drove me forward into the life I have now. And from a distance, that can look like grace. Twenty years ago, I might have described myself with that word, mistaking it as a synonym for *politeness*. Now I know better. Now, I understand what it means to live with grace.

In my experience, grace softens the edges of other characteristics. Grace drapes itself over each thought and word, cushioning interactions by easing sharp corners. Grace invites others to trust. When I think of grace, I think of the glow of candlelight and how tiny flames can transform a room, making it feel safe and welcoming. That is how I understand grace. And I can still remember the first time that I felt that gentle light on my skin, and softened under its comforting attention. It was surprising and pleasant. It felt like being accepted without saying a word. It felt like love.

***

I was in love when I experienced grace for the first time. I had been dating Peter, a man I worked with, for a few months. It was tentative as I had just finalized my divorce and Peter was in the process of finalizing his. We hadn't said *I love you* yet, but I could feel the words bubbling in me, exciting and comforting at the same time. I was in Portland, Oregon, working as a business manager at a plastics company, and while planning a trip to the head office in Calgary, Peter made the fateful suggestion that I stay with his parents. I hesitated not only out of fear of imposing myself on strangers but also because we hadn't told anyone we were seeing each other.

"My mom loves having houseguests, and you could get to know both of them a little," Peter said. I was hesitant but looked forward to meeting the mother he spoke of so affectionately. I accepted Peter's offer even though he wouldn't be there as he'd been planning a canoe trip down the Nahanni River in the Northwest Territories for months. He called his mother and told her to expect me, and a few weeks later, there I was, welcomed into their condo and their lives.

After our first introduction, Grace invited me in. "I'm Grace, and you know, that's Bob." Peter's father said "Hi, Connie" and shook my hand firmly. He was a career military man, and although I knew him to be a warm person, I was sometimes taken aback by his intimidating presence. The fact that Bob remembered my name from our one and only work conference put me at ease. He took my small bag as they led me in.

"How was the flight?" Grace asked. I waved my hand and explained that I flew about as often as I drove, or so it seemed. Grace smiled easily at me. "Would you like a drink, or something to eat?" she asked.

I laughed a little and took off my coat. "Just some water would be great, thanks," I responded.

Grace directed me to go into the living room as she turned back to the kitchen, where I could hear her pulling glasses out of a cupboard. I sat down on the love seat and was surprised at how comfortable it was. I wriggled around and settled my back properly against the cushions, feeling immediately more at ease. From the kitchen, Grace shut the cupboard door. The noise of clinking glass moved toward me, and Grace began to speak. "I have a glass of water for you," she said as she came around the corner, "but I thought you might help me with this bottle of wine. Only if you'd like, of course!" She smiled as she set down the tray, loaded with two wine glasses and a glass of water and a plate with crackers, cheese, and little purple grapes. There were two linen napkins folded in the middle. Peter was right; Grace was quite the hostess but not in a way that made me worry about which fork to use. I felt at ease.

"Honestly, I'd love some wine. Thank you, Grace," I said.

"Well, Peter assured me you were wonderful company. He told me that you are so funny, just a pleasure to work with," she responded. She smiled as she settled into the seat beside me, thinking about Peter. I smiled as well at my good fortune in being so well taken care of.

Peter knew that I would have fun staying with Grace and Bob, but I hadn't been sure until I'd seen Grace come around the corner with the wine. I could tell she wanted us to be friends, that she was pleased to have me here. Being welcomed so genuinely was not something I had expected, but it was exactly what I needed, especially while Peter was away. I was supportive of him going on this trip; he loved adventures in snow and ice; he loved sailboats, climbing, and skiing, anything with a little risk to it. I learned quickly after our first meeting that the photos on his wall represented only a few of the adventures he'd commandeered for himself. He was an adventurer cloaked in a business suit. I loved his enthusiasm and his daring right away; we shared the same instinct to rush at each day and accomplish big things. This trip was the first time we had been out of touch for more than a day or two, and as I went about my daily life without him, I had the faint sense that I had lost some of my speed. It was as if I had gotten so used to the energy of our combined enthusiasm that moving under my own steam didn't feel the same. I missed the momentum that Peter sparked in me. I missed Peter. Finding a friend in Grace felt very natural, in part because she loved Peter like I did. Not that I said it to her. Not that I said that to anyone.

That evening, long after Bob had retired to his study to read, Grace and I traced our histories and traded our maps of home with each other. I was surprised at how well she could evoke each city in her past through memory. She had crisscrossed the United States in her lifetime before settling in Canada. Her narrative of each place reflected the person she was when she lived there. Her childhood was spent in Dividend, a tiny coal mining town in Utah that is now a ghost town. When she talked about chasing grasshoppers with brooms for entertainment and the crowded one-room schoolhouse where she attended classes, her early restlessness emerged in her voice. She explained how stifled she felt by the monotony of the rocky yellow hills. Her family moved to Salt Lake City when she was a teenager, and her whole face brightened when she told me about the thrill of being in, what seemed by comparison, a huge city. "After isolation in Dividend," she said, "what I wanted was some company, for me and for my sisters! There were tram cars and stores where I could get a job." The Second World War brought her a chance to experience life on an even larger stage. At age twenty-one, she left Utah, taking the bus to San Francisco where she got a job working as a secretary at the Treasure Island Naval Base. She dubbed her few months living there with her friend Donna as her "single days." "There were nightclubs, music, and dancing. Nothing like Utah," she described brightly.

When I pressed for more details, Grace laughed a little. "There's no more to tell, Connie. I met Bob in the office one afternoon, and that was it! We were married three weeks later. Bob was sent off to war on one of the ships from the base, and Bob's mother brought me to Beverly Hills as soon as she knew I was pregnant." Grace had Pamela while living with her mother-in-law, and then, when the war ended and Bob came home, Grace moved again.

Grace had Peter, her first son, while living in a suburb in Los Angeles. It is the place where her identity as wife and mother became real for her. She told me about the nursery she decorated using her own sewing machine, the Christmases when Bob would play Santa to surprise the kids, the park around the corner from their house where the other mothers would congregate and talk, sometimes openly and sometimes in hushed voices, about their lives. Grace leaned in a little to explain to me. "I was always careful not to say much. Bob was a military man and didn't like the idea of me trading secrets about him. But I did like being in that circle. We traded dress patterns and recipes—I even learned how to mix drinks. Bob didn't mind that lesson—I'd bring him gin martinis when he got in from work!" She threw her eyes to the ceiling in an exaggerated gesture, remembering the pride of that accomplishment, and I laughed at her theatricality, entranced by the world she was narrating for me. It felt good to be Grace's audience; it felt like we were recreating that circle of women gathered in the park. It was clear from Grace's easy expression that her time there had suited her very well.

"Next we came to Virginia, but we weren't there for long. It couldn't have been more than three years . . ." Grace paused as her eyes looked past me, trying to reclaim details of her time in Virginia. "Bob was working for the Pentagon then, and I thought there'd be a nice little community of military wives there, but really, we had barely settled in when we made a major change in our lives.

"I remember being so surprised when Bob came home one afternoon and said that the next stop was Calgary, Canada. It was still the early days of an oil boom in Alberta, and Bob was leaving the military to join his father in a start-up oil venture. It took a second for me to register it, and my first thought was that I wasn't sure I could pick it out on a map! I mean, it was starting to become a proper city, but only just. I wouldn't have ever picked it as a place to live back then. I thought to myself, give it a few years, we'll see how long this lasts but look! We're still here more than forty years later!" She shook her head with a smile and settled herself again on the couch. "All the kids think of Calgary as home. That's a strange thing. They know this place better than they know Utah or California—the places that I think of as my original home. But Canada has been good to this family."

For the first time in the conversation, there was a proper pause, and Grace sighed softly. Forgetting about me for a moment, she seemed to be contemplating her last statements. I could see Grace thinking about how far her children's home, a place of ice and snow in a modern city built on the juncture of prairies and mountains, was from her own first home, a dusty mining town dug into the Utah hills. I understood this divide. I knew the feeling of having traveled too far from home; I was the child who had been gone too long to ever return to the place I had once called home. I sat still on the couch with Grace, thinking about her and about my mother, knowing that there was nothing I could say. I remember that moment very clearly, that first moment I felt Grace and I had built a bond. Her story about the places she had lived seemed innocuous enough when we first started chatting, glasses of wine in our hands, but once she started letting her memories lead her narration, she left herself exposed. Having moved as many times as I had, I knew the difference between the places we go and the places we live. I knew that mapping out home is always a tricky effort. Home happens when we find a connection—to ourselves, to family, sometimes to total strangers. Home is a place where memories, hopes, and fears are unpacked along with everything else.

It was quiet in Grace and Bob's living room as we sat, held by different thoughts on the same theme, and it suddenly occurred to me how comfortable I felt. I had known Grace only a short time, and yet, here we were, sitting together and talking as if we were old friends. I felt powerfully welcome, like a long-awaited guest. It wasn't what I had expected when Peter suggested this visit.

During that long first conversation, Grace and I never mentioned Peter. We talked around him easily, so easily that I didn't even notice we were doing it. It was late by the time we stopped chatting, and Grace bundled me up to bed before going back downstairs to clean up the dishes. I prepared for bed and set my alarm for the next morning. It had been a great night. But as I looked out the bedroom window at the lights on the building across from me, I wished I could talk to Peter and tell him what a wonder his mother was, what it meant to me to find a stranger transform herself into a friend so easily. I wanted to tell him that Grace reminded me of him. She was much quieter than Peter, but when she was telling stories, there was the same brightness in her eyes and the same energy in her fingers. He had her warmth too. And sitting alone without either of them, I felt my own energy and enthusiasm dip low.

I was lost in thought about Peter when there was a hushed knock at my door. I wiped my face as if I'd been crying, although I hadn't, and cleared my throat quietly before standing up to answer the door. "Are you still awake, dear?" asked Grace. I eased the door open and the light from the hallway slanted into the room. Grace was standing in front of me with an atlas. She smiled at me sweetly, and then her eyes seemed to twinkle. "I thought," she began as she came into the room, "that we might see if we can't find where Peter is on one of these maps." She settled on the bed, and holding the book in her right hand, she patted the quilt with her left. I sat down beside her, hip to hip, as she opened the cover and started flipping pages. While she flipped from one country to the next, she talked about what Peter had been like as a boy, always running, always rushing. Her stream of chatter made me realize I was holding my breath. I wanted to see the page he was on; I wanted to feel connected to him in some direct way. As trivial as it was, I wanted to find him on that map. Grace found the page revealing the Northwest Territories, and we both leaned in, peering over the tiny fonts on the page.

After a moment, Grace pulled back just a little, and the book slid toward me, just a matter of inches. When I saw the words *Nahanni River*, I felt a soft relief. "It's there, it's there!" I whispered to Grace.

"Let's see," she said, and we leaned back over the map again, my finger tracing the route Peter had explained to me before he left. Grace laughed quietly. "Our Peter sure does love to travel," she said to me as she folded up the book.

"Yes," I said calmly, feeling irrationally settled for having seen the map. I didn't even notice that she had used the word *our*.

Grace stood up and put the atlas on the dresser, and then turned back to me. She took my hand and placed it between her own two hands. "Sleep well, Connie," she said, smiling just a little. "I'll see you in the morning." I nodded, still half-thinking about Peter.

When she got to the door, I spoke again. "Grace?" She paused and turned back to me, so I continued. "Thank you for such excellent company." It wasn't what I wanted to say, but it was all I could manage in the moment.

Grace shook her head gently. "Of course, Connie. It was my pleasure."

I think about that first night with Grace a lot. It felt like the three of us—Grace, Peter, and I—formed a little triumvirate that night. Grace and Peter were a unit, Peter and I were becoming a unit, and then, after a night of chatting, I found myself bonded to Grace as well. It has always felt like Grace understood me. She could tell I was in love with Peter by the way I talked about him and the way I didn't talk about him. And she suspected Peter was in love as well by the way that he would casually mention me to her when they were talking about work, or the weather, or his new hiking shoes. Grace has always been very perceptive. She became my confidant on the first night that we met, consoling me without saying a word. Since then, she has become my mother, my sister, my best friend.

Chapter Two

The Temptation of Hindsight

Hindsight promises to explain how our lives unfold, to clarify patterns that we didn't see the first time. And while many of us crave this clarity, hindsight can be a burden. Hindsight lacks context. It might sharpen our understanding of the past, but as a path drawn in reverse, hindsight doesn't show all the false starts and the wrong turns we took in our efforts to find a path forward. Hindsight can be disingenuous; it suggests that there was a path to be followed even when we couldn't see it. The fact remains that there is never a clear path as we move through life. We fumble and struggle, and when we find our way, hindsight reminds us of each mistake we made. As if every wrong turn didn't help to create the path itself.

The question "How did I miss this?" is a dangerous one. These words sound like an indictment, as if it is always possible to extrapolate the whole from the fragments of truth that we can see. So many of us are failed detectives. We are taught to hold back until we know enough, to find proof before making accusations. We learn early in life that false conclusions can cause harm. And so we gather evidence, piece by piece, and wait until we have built our case, first for ourselves and then for others. We wait until we are sure of being right. And if we wait too long, we blame ourselves for being afraid.

I feel anxious when I look back through my life for evidence of the things I failed to understand. That kind of introspection makes me see my life as a series of missteps. Worse, it makes me suspect I am still missing important details. I watch myself juggle the elements of my life and worry that I've missed other details, that there are other surprises waiting for me in the future. And since the day when Grace was diagnosed with Alzheimer's disease, I've spent a lot of time thinking about the past and wondering where hindsight's path should start and end.

***

At the moment of Grace's diagnosis, as I was sitting in the specialist's office, all I could think was that I had made a significant error. Dr. Gaede's confident assessment told me that the signs of the disease were clear and in place, and having him confirm my suspicions so easily made me feel that I had failed to see the obvious sooner. Why had I waited so long before I finally walked into the doctor's office, my arm linked in Grace's arm, with all her documents in my purse?

As a family, we had all begun to see worrying signs. Over Christmas a few months previously, Peter, Pamela, and I had discussed the changes we were seeing in Grace, and we agreed we should get a referral to a doctor in Palm Desert, where Grace lived in the winter. We had traded comments about Grace's forgetfulness and anxiety over the year prior, but we hadn't discussed it as a group until the holidays gathered us all together.

Although Bob had passed away a few years earlier, the house had been crowded and lively as holiday homecomings can be. Peter's three children from his first marriage were there, along with Pam's family. Late one night, after the kids had settled into bed and the house was quiet, we sat down at the kitchen table and confirmed one another's observations. Yes, Grace had seemed confused today, asking about the gifts we had opened the day before. Yes, she had taken a long time to get dressed today, insisting that someone had rearranged her closet and moved her favorite dress. Yes, we had all seen her standing beside Peter, patting his arm but fumbling for his name for just a second. There was agreement around the table, which was, in one sense, a relief, even if the conclusions we were drawing were worrying. Being huddled around the table with Peter and Pamela made me feel like I had found allies. I was tired of questioning myself, of wondering if Grace's small missteps were any more than the realities of being eighty-three years old. Hearing Peter and Pamela trade observations, watching one nod as the other spoke, I felt more sure of my perceptions, better prepared to move forward. But in that same moment, I also felt a new burden descend—the need to act even though I feared the next step was not an easy one. I knew no matter what we discovered, there would be consequences; changes would be required and adjustments would need to be made. This discussion marked the day that we admitted to ourselves that the changes we were seeing in Grace were serious, and that was significant. We would not be able to backtrack.

We agreed that we needed a consultation with an expert so that we could be sure of what we were dealing with. We agreed that we needed to keep a record of Grace's behavior so that we could spot patterns. In my mind, there was a long list of things we needed to set in place, of actions we needed to take. The organized businesswoman in me wanted to make a physical list, to turn the conversation into a plan we could follow and review. Because I seemed ready, the others deferred to me, and soon enough, the list was mine to keep. I was glad of it because it gave me something to do, some way to control my feelings. In truth, I was frightened to death.

The prospect of Alzheimer's disease scared me. Dementia scared me. In part, it was that I didn't know enough to face these prospects like I had faced cancer. At least cancer is factual, tangible. At least the process is clear: testing, diagnosis, treatment. We had sat at this same table seven years earlier, in 1996, discussing Bob's cancer.

Bob had taken his diagnosis with a stiff upper lip and kept his fears, and later his pain, to himself. He answered questions stoically and insisted that he was fine. Once Bob had closed a conversation, it was closed. Respecting his wishes, I found myself primarily dealing with his illness through Grace. When Peter and I would visit Grace and Bob, we'd peel off into two groups, Peter and Bob holing up in the den while Grace and I settled ourselves at the kitchen table. Privately, Grace channeled information through me to her children, reaching out to them in a way Bob couldn't. Grace told me when she saw cracks in his armor when he seemed despondent or angry. After fifty years of marriage, Bob was determined not to burden Grace with his fears, but he underestimated how well Grace could read him, how savvy she could be. It was a matter of pride for Bob that his cancer didn't disrupt the rest of the family, and it seemed to me that he held himself apart so that no one would pry too deeply into his feelings about the disease.

Grace shared small details about Bob with me as I sat across from her at the kitchen table, and while she maintained the party line that everything was going to be fine during the early stages of the treatment, there were times when her confidence would falter, her assurances ending with question marks. Bob's cancer brought Grace and me closer together because I helped her to have the conversations that she couldn't have with Bob. What she needed was to be honest about what was happening and be reassured that we would deal with the outcome together. At the end of our chats, the lines around Grace's eyes would soften and she would sit still in her chair, her eyes drifting a little, as I gathered up the mugs and cleared the counter.

My instinct says cancer is an easier disease than Alzheimer's because there are more facts, fewer questions, but in truth, it had more to do with the circumstances. With Bob's cancer, Grace was there to help me understand the situation, to know what to do and when. Grace let me feel strong by being her confidant, but if she were the one that was sick, my source of support would be constantly slipping away. Grace couldn't be my compass through this illness. Thinking about how Grace and I had leaned on one another to get through Bob's cancer, I realized that I was scared to face the prospect of Alzheimer's disease without Grace. I didn't want to feel alone, and I didn't want her to feel alone either.

Despite that fear, I knew that we needed to find a way forward. So I did. "I'll make an appointment with Dr. Gaede," I said, my voice sure and strong. "We can get Grace in for an evaluation and we can go from there. We aren't even sure that he'll find anything. But we need to know. We can't do anything until we have knowledge." I'd found Dr. Gaede's name while doing some halfhearted research about Alzheimer's, telling myself that I was just preparing for the future. I said we were fortunate there was a specialist in our area and that our family had enough resources to manage the medical hurdles we could expect to face. Peter and Pamela nodded in agreement, and that was it. I think we all felt better after that conversation, knowing that we were taking some positive steps. With more confidence than anyone probably really felt, we affirmed that, together, we could handle whatever the appointment revealed. When I made the appointment for Grace, I told myself wishfully that this appointment was a checkup to rule out a problem rather than to confirm it.

I didn't tell Grace exactly what we were doing when we went to see Dr. Gaede. Peter had returned to Canada for work and Pamela had gone home to Santa Fe. Even if they had been available, it seemed easier and more natural for me to take her by myself. I didn't want to worry her, and more honestly, I didn't want to embarrass her without need. I had been planning my approach for several days and decided since, as we didn't know anything yet, there was no need to unnerve her with the specter of Alzheimer's disease. I didn't want to discredit her ability or undermine her confidence. And so I told her we were going for a doctor's appointment and left it at that. Grace smiled at me as we settled in the car and told me that I looked well put together. She always had an eye for fashion and still dressed herself up before leaving the house. I laughed a little and squeezed her hand, feeling glad for her good mood and nervous for the afternoon we were facing. As I backed the car out, I wondered if I shouldn't just tell her where we were going. Maybe this approach wasn't kinder; maybe not being candid about our concerns would just make Grace feel like an incapable old woman. I knew Grace so well, but I had no strong sense of how she would react to this.

As we sat at a red light, only a few minutes into our drive, Grace turned to me, suddenly anxious. "I don't have my purse, Connie. I don't have it. I must have forgotten it at the house!" The muscles of her face were knit together, and her forehead was creased with concern. Her tone suggested fear, not exasperation. She craned her neck back in the direction of the house, and as she looked, she asked, "Can we go back? Connie?"

"Isn't it?" I scanned the floor in front of her to see the purse but it wasn't there. The lights changed, and I pulled my eyes back onto the road, moving through the lights and signalling a lane change, slowing to find a spot along the road to park the car. "All right, Grace, it's no problem, hang on," I said, trying to settle her nerves. She didn't respond. I eased the car into a narrow spot along the sidewalk and turned off the engine. "Didn't we both have our purses when we left?" I asked, thinking hard. "Didn't we put them in the backseat?" I leaned back between our two front seats and surveyed the seats, the floor, and sure enough, our purses.

I fished Grace's purse strap from my own and hauled it up for her. Seeing her purse, Grace visibly relaxed and reached for it. "Did we?

I guess we did. I'm sorry, Connie, I just hate being out without my purse."

I smiled at her, glad to see this tiny crisis averted. "Well, they did slide almost under the seat—it's good that you thought to double-check!" I said, seeking to smooth her brow and return her calm.

Grace settled both hands across the bag as I started the car and slid back into traffic. I put on some music and left Grace to sit quietly, wanting to give her time to settle before we got to the doctor's office. I hated seeing Grace work herself up over something so minor, but our exchange answered the question I had been asking myself minutes earlier. I was right to say nothing; we all were. What Grace needed was clarity, not confusing speculation.

When we got to the office, Grace sat patiently beside me as I filled out the paperwork. "Will we go in together?" she asked.

"I think so," I responded, thankful once again for Grace's good nature. If she ever got the sense she could help, she would help. The waiting room was small and nicely furnished, and the receptionist was friendly. I was glad for the sense of calm in the office because I didn't feel calm at all. It had been easier before we made the appointment, before we had come here. At home, I batted away the idea that Grace might be seriously sick every time we sat down for dinner and chatted, every time she made a joke and laughed along with me, tickled at her cleverness. But now, sitting in Dr. Gaede's office, all I could think about was Grace's confusion about her purse and her panic at being without it. When I thought about going to the doctor's office, my nerves were easier to brush away, but while waiting for Dr. Gaede's door to open, I felt sharply on edge. I've never been the type to avoid problems; I've always waited stoically for bad news or punishment. Hiding didn't solve anything, and so I didn't hide now as much as I might have liked to. In that waiting room, I thought about how strong Grace had been during Bob's cancer. Grace deserved my best support, my confidence and assurances. She didn't need my fear. And so I sat tall and took a deep breath. Leaning in toward Grace, I made a joke about the article she was reading in one of the waiting room magazines and laughed with her when she laughed. And when the receptionist called our names and indicated the office at the end of the hall, I smiled at Grace, took her hand, and walked with her into the next stage of her life.

Dr. Gaede was well practiced at putting people at ease. He introduced himself to Grace and then to me, and as I braced myself for the interview to begin, he leaned forward and said gently, "Grace, your kids have told me that there is a problem with your memory." It was like an expertly delivered needle, so quick and painless that I wasn't sure it had happened. His tone was neutral, his face open. I felt a rush of confidence but then looked at Grace and felt my confidence disappear again.

Her face was tight, her fists gripping the leather straps of her purse. I heard the silence tick by as Grace glared at Dr. Gaede, insulted by the question, and then turned to me, accusingly. "So you've been talking to *him* behind my back? Accusing me and telling lies?" I glanced up at Dr. Gaede, not sure whether to respond or stay silent. As I considered what to say, afraid to admit what we were all afraid of, Grace reached forward and banged her fist against the desk. "How dare you, Connie! How dare you drag me in here to be evaluated like this without any discussion? I am not a child! I won't be treated this way!" Her voice was shrill and loud, cutting through the room, but Dr. Gaede's expression hadn't changed at all. To my relief, he responded to Grace, describing our concerns, explaining our actions. He spoke about memory problems without mentioning Alzheimer's disease at all and talked about warning signs and aging. As he spoke, Grace shot me bitter glances and glared at me accusingly while answering the doctor's questions. To him, she was curt, but it was clear that she blamed me for the situation. Once, when he pushed her to clarify one of her answers, she glared at him for a moment before she frostily evaded his inquiry. He wove his evaluative test questions into their conversation so neatly, I didn't know which questions were conversational and which were diagnostic. In less than twenty minutes, he had what he needed from Grace. He glanced at me and nodded to let me know he was finished and then leaned in toward Grace and thanked her for their chat. He asked her if he could talk to me alone and saw her to the door, pointing her toward the waiting room and watching as she walked down the hall. As soon as Grace's seat was empty, my body clenched. I had been so focused on Grace during the conversation that the sudden reality of this new situation caught me off guard. The conversation had been the easy part; the hard part would begin now. As the doctor closed the door and turned back to me, I tried to be friendly, but my conversation felt hollow. I was afraid I was about to lose something very precious to me.

Dr. Gaede looked at me kindly. "You and Grace are quite close," he observed. "That is good. That will make things easier." I felt a lurch as those words settled in my ears, like my body had been momentarily imbalanced. I nodded. "Connie, I'm afraid that the news isn't good. I see several of the classic signs of Alzheimer's disease in Grace's behavior and response pattern." He paused and looked down at the notes he had scrawled during his interview with Grace. His observation hung in the air, and I felt my mind collapse into a jumble of ribbons. Despair grabbed at me. For three seconds, I felt myself collapse. But three seconds was all I could allow myself. I nodded at Dr. Gaede as the ribbons in my mind pulled taut. A deep breath swallowed everything whole, and suddenly I was calm, focused. Suddenly, all I could see was the task at hand, and I threw myself at that task, for Grace, for the family. And for myself. Trying to control the hurt, I pulled out a notebook and a pen and started to write. Dr. Gaede paused, giving me time to breathe again, and then he started to explain. He started by pulling examples from his chat with Grace. "Did you notice that she evaded my question about her weekend? It's common for Alzheimer's patients to struggle with recent memories more than long-term memories. She remembers first meeting you, but not having dinner with you last night. And the evasion is part of the diagnosis as well. Alzheimer's patients typically hide lapses in memory by offering other facts or details. When I pushed her, she got frustrated. It's because she couldn't find a way out without admitting she didn't know, and she wouldn't admit that."

I nodded as I pulled out the key terms and wrote them hastily on the page. "I didn't realize. She does that a lot—evade me, I mean—and I didn't realize it was a symptom. I thought she was just getting older, and I didn't want to push her and make her self-conscious. I didn't want to make it harder . . ." My voice fell away as I realized what I was saying didn't matter. Now was not the time for recrimination.

Dr. Gaede smiled kindly and shook his head. "Connie, this is a complicated disease. It looks a lot like aging in some ways." I didn't want him to excuse me; I didn't want to become the focus of the conversation, so I asked what else he saw in Grace. "The frustration is important because it's part of a shift in the id, in how Grace operates with other people. As the disease develops, she is more likely to get angry. Her emotions will sometimes seem erratic. As you know her well, you will see these changes and that can help us map the progression." I wrote down the word *anger* but I drew a box around it, separating it from the other symptoms on the list. I couldn't imagine Grace as an angry person. Her reaction today was unusual for her, and I understood exactly why she was upset. I skipped down the page and started writing again, ignoring the word *anger*.

". . . sentence salad," said Dr. Gaede. I looked up at him, confused by the term, having missed the sentence before. Dr. Gaede smiled gently, and started again, explaining how some of Grace's responses to his questions seemed correct, but were only superficially on topic, suggesting that she was having problems understanding the questions. "She's covering, and she's covering well, but the fundamental problem remains. It will get harder for her to cover over the gaps in her thinking, and she will become increasingly aware of that. She's likely to have a lot of negative emotions about that as things get worse. And she's likely to blame others for her errors. It's a matter of self-preservation."

The word *self-preservation* rang in my mind. As I wrote it down on the page, I suddenly understood something about the disease that had eluded me before this meeting. It clicked in my mind that Grace was in the midst of a battle and that she had been battling it alone for some time. As much as she had been fighting the disease, she was also fighting to protect all of us. As she was losing ground in her memory, she was struggling to keep us from noticing. The disease was the first front of the battle, and we were the second front. Being as close as we were must only have made that fight harder for her. The idea of Grace in a silent and lonely war pained me. I felt emotion kick up, but my brain forced it into retreat. I had to stay in this moment. I cleared my throat and looked up again. "So you think this has been going on for a while?"

Dr. Gaede paused and then sighed. When he answered, he spoke quietly. "Yes, Connie. A long while." He paused again, and watched me with steady eyes as I nodded and swallowed hard.

"So, months . . . ?" My voice trailed off as I thought back over the past six months, trying to pick out the moments that I should have seen signs.

His voice interrupted me. "Years, Connie. Years. Likely, the disease began to show symptoms when Grace was in her seventies, and has been progressing steadily since then."

He turned away to reach for a book on the shelf behind him as I floundered, trying to understand his meaning. I had met Grace almost a decade ago. Had it been happening then? Had I been missing the signs all this time? My throat tightened. I felt my body sag like so much dough; my breath muffled in my chest. How could we not have seen it; how could I not have seen . . . ? "You have to remember, the evidence of this disease presents differently in each patient, and it can be hard to diagnose in the early stages. The symptoms are often similar to the normal stages of aging. A lot of the patients I see for the first time are in advanced stages of the disease, like Grace."

I nodded, gripping my pen tightly. I tracked his words like a beacon in the dark. "So . . ." I began and then paused. My voice was a little shrill, and I didn't trust it to last. "Advanced stage?"

"It seems so, yes. Grace has the usual symptoms of late-stage Alzheimer's disease. There are some symptoms that I don't see evidence of, but there is enough in her behavior for a conclusive diagnosis." Dr. Gaede gestured to some pamphlets on the corner of his desk, and I leaned in to take several.

"Isn't there some sort of test? Blood work?" I asked, clutching at the idea that there might still be a reprieve for Grace. The pamphlets seemed flimsy in my hand, not at all sufficient to help me understand this news.

"There are some tests, yes, but behavioral diagnosis is considered a standard approach, especially with someone at Grace's age. She is presenting with all the usual symptoms, and her medical history doesn't indicate any other likely cause of the changes that she is experiencing. I know it is hard to hear, Connie, but you came here knowing there was a problem, and I'm telling you, the cause is Alzheimer's disease." He spoke the words so matter-of-factly that I nodded, suddenly accepting this revelation. Suddenly feeling that, if I didn't accept it, it would get away from me, and I wouldn't be able to help Grace at all.

I flipped to a new page in my notebook and looked up expectantly. "What do we do now?" I asked. "For Grace. What do I do?"

Dr. Gaede looked across the table at me and then settled back in his smooth leather chair. He glanced out the window at the light spraying through the leaves of the trees outside his office. "Now comes the hard part, Connie." I inwardly cringed, wondering what could be harder than bearing this news without tears, frantic and hot. My pen stayed poised, but my shoulders slid low. "Now, you become the patient,

Connie. We need to make a plan for you." I leaned forward and wrote my name at the top of the page and then faltered. I must have misheard. I looked up and saw kindness in his face. He continued. "Alzheimer's disease is not like most other diseases. There is no treatment. There is nothing we can do to stop it from progressing. All we can do is manage Grace's symptoms and help her to live as fully as possible. What Grace needs now is a strong caregiver, and that means you. You and whoever else will be caring for Grace." For the first time, I thought beyond myself and Grace. Sitting in this office, my world had shrunk to just Grace and me, but suddenly, I saw Peter's face in front of me and Pamela's as well. I saw Peter's girls, Chelsea, Lindsey, and Katie, crowded around Grace, all smiling. The idea of having to share this news with them was overwhelming. I had so many questions of my own, and I had no answers. I had no idea how this diagnosis was going to change our lives. I didn't know how to say the words *Alzheimer's disease* without scaring us all.

Dr. Gaede must have seen this on my face because he sat forward in his chair and reached across the desk. I extended a hand toward his, and he squeezed it gently. "It's normal to feel overwhelmed, Connie. I know this is going to be the start of some major changes for you and your family. But this isn't as confusing as it feels right now." His tone was confident and kind. His hand was comforting. I sat up tall in the chair and took a breath. In my mind, I could see the faces of my family, and among them, Grace's sweet smile and her delicate crinkly eyes. I focused on her face and on Dr. Gaede's last words. It's better to know, I thought. It's important that we know so we can be the best for Grace. That thought made sense and helped to settle me.

I looked at Dr. Gaede and nodded. "Thank you." Our hands slid apart and I settled back into the chair. "This is . . . we didn't think that . . . I just . . ." It seemed unnecessary to finish my sentence.

Dr. Gaede waved it away with his hand and sat back as well. "It might be helpful if I spoke to Grace's children, and to whoever will be caring for Grace. I'm happy to do a conference call and address all of the family's concerns. Having everyone on the same page will make this easier for you, and for Grace." I nodded, feeling relief. I had brought Grace to the office alone, and though Peter and Pamela had each instructed me to call as soon as I could with the result, the idea of calling them once Grace and I got back to her house in Palm Desert scared me. They would have questions, and I would have nothing but fear and disappointment to offer them. How could I tell Grace's children this? I didn't know, and I was palpably terrified at the prospect of having to find a way. "If you think they would be available now . . . ?" Dr. Gaede offered, and I nodded again before leaning forward in the chair to write their numbers on the notebook he offered me.

I watched as his fingers punched in the numbers firmly. He looked up at me just as he hit the loudspeaker button, and I jumped a little as the ringing began. Peter answered quickly as if he'd been waiting for the call, and I felt relieved as his steady voice filled the room. Dr. Gaede introduced himself and explained about the conference call. I could picture Peter at the other end, nodding as the doctor spoke, and I wished for a moment that I hadn't insisted on making this visit alone. After a pause, Peter's voice filled the room again. "Connie? Are you . . . ?"

I could hear a slight strain in his tone, and the urge to reassure him that I was all right pushed me forward in my chair. "I'm here, Peter. I'm okay."

I heard him exhale, and after a pause, he echoed me. "Okay. Okay."

Dr. Gaede nodded at me and turned his attention back to the phone, putting Peter on hold while he dialed Pamela's number. As the slight buzz of Peter's office was replaced with a dial tone, I realized how much his voice on the other end of the line meant to me. I breathed deeply and closed my eyes, wishing I could lean against his shoulder and feel my hands held between his. The memory of that comfort made me smile, and knowing that he would be listening and questioning right here with me, I felt some of my tension drop away. A minute later, Pamela's voice came over the line, expectant. I listened as Dr. Gaede introduced himself and then I offered a quick hello as Peter was brought back into the conversation. Dr. Gaede started talking, explaining his diagnosis and the symptoms that were most indicative of Alzheimer's disease. Listening to him was soothing; I was able to understand more of what he said now that the shock was wearing off. Knowing that Peter and Pamela were listening with me in that room made it easier as well. I piped up with comments every so often, steering the conversation toward practical matters or restating things I remembered from my earlier conversation with the doctor. But for the most part, I listened. I listened to Pamela's questions about other causes and other possible reasons for Grace's confusion. I heard her holding the diagnosis at arm's length until Dr. Gaede affirmed that this was the only diagnosis that fit. Then she shifted. Accepting the diagnosis, she wanted strategies; she wanted a way forward. I listened for Peter, quiet, his boisterousness lost under the weight of this news. He didn't ask questions. His silence told me that he felt out of his depth, unsure. The longer he was quiet, the more I interjected. Talking about Grace's involvement in her own treatment, I echoed Dr. Gaede's feeling that we needed to let Grace set the pace for further action. When we discussed Grace's living alone, I pushed to let Grace keep moving between Palm Desert and Calgary, believing it was worthwhile to maintain her routine. I wanted to keep everything as normal as possible, for all of us. I didn't want Grace's world to suddenly shrink; I didn't want to lose more of Grace than I already had.

While we were formulating a plan to manage Grace's illness, it occurred to me that we were also trying to control the changes this disease would entail. Dr. Gaede lead the conversation, falling silent to hear the concerns, the projections, the speculations of a family grappling with a problem we couldn't yet clearly comprehend. His opinions helped to cement proposals into action; his presence inspired confidence. We talked until no one had any questions left to ask. Promising that he would be available for further discussion, we hung up, and he turned back to me. "Do you feel better now?" he asked.

I smiled. This disease still terrified me, but collaborating with Pamela and Peter made me feel more confident, better prepared. It didn't feel like the weight was all on my shoulders, like this was my crisis to manage alone. "Yes, I really do. Thank you so much for your time. It is so appreciated by all of us." Saying this, I felt relief flood over me, genuine calm settling in. The words *Alzheimer's disease* scared me. The words made Grace disappear; all I could see was the disease and a future of watching that disease take Grace away from me. But now, I felt clear again. I remembered that Grace hadn't changed because of the diagnosis, that she was still the same woman she had been this morning.

I gathered my things and Dr. Gaede and I walked through the door and into the hallway. Turning, I extended my hand to shake his. "Thanks again. I'll be in touch to set up a home visit between you and Grace," I said.

Dr. Gaede smiled and nodded. "You call my office if you have any questions." I felt a dart of nerves in my stomach as I looked down the hall toward the waiting room. He leaned closer to me. "You've been her caregiver all this time, and you've done a good job. Nothing has changed."

I let the words hang, wanting to hear them again. Wanting to believe them. "Thank you," I said, confused by the term *caregiver*. Had I been caring for Grace without knowing it? Could I really just keep doing what I'd always done? It didn't seem like enough to be her friend, knowing what I now knew. But where else would I start?

At the waiting room, I stopped, seeing Grace thumbing quietly through a thick fashion magazine. When she looked up at me, she crinkled her nose, tilted the magazine toward me, and gestured toward a photo. "Not at all a flattering hemline, in my opinion!" she offered, then dropping the magazine on the side table and gathering her purse. "You certainly were in there a long time—are you okay?" She peered at my face, concern written on her brow. Inwardly, there I felt chaos. Love and grief battled in my heart, and I couldn't temper either of them.

In part to assuage my fear and in part to hide my face, I put my arms around her and held her close to me. After a moment, I spoke in a bright voice. "Of course, but I missed you!"

Grace rubbed my back like she had a hundred times before and laughed her delicate laugh. When she pulled away, I was more sure of my smile. "Didn't you say we'd go for lunch after this appointment?" Grace asked. I nodded, powerfully pleased at her memory of this promise. Tea between friends seemed like a good place to start this new path. And with that, Grace took my hand and we turned to the door, heading out into the bright sunshine.

That night, while the television scattered light across the living room and I stared at the screen without really watching, hindsight began to haunt me. The idea of Alzheimer's disease began to rattle me again. The diagnosis had been so quick, so easy. In those few minutes, Grace's life, and my life, had become disoriented. Questions began to echo faintly in my mind, like a voice calling from a deep cave, quiet but fervent, demanding my attention. "Why didn't you see it? Why didn't you protect her?" The longer I thought, the more the voice became impossible to ignore. Closing my eyes, I let my mind freefall, directed by the questions I didn't have answers to. Dr. Gaede said Grace had likely been losing ground since I met her, so it didn't matter where I looked at this point. I had no memory of Grace that the disease wasn't present. The realization defeated me. In my mind, this diagnosis took something from Grace that I wasn't willing to let go of. When I thought about Alzheimer's patients, I imagined confused, frustrated people, lost in their own lives. Grace was not like that; she was never like that. She was sweet, caring, insightful. As I stood nervously in her hallway the first day that I met her, she had taken my hand in both of hers and calmed me. I examined the moment in my mind but saw nothing other than a lovely, vibrant person. I didn't know how to trace the early symptoms of Alzheimer's disease in my foundational memories of Grace. It made me uncomfortable to try; I was afraid that I might unintentionally unsettle something of myself in trying to see the shadow of the disease in her actions.

So much of my life has been built around Peter's family. Being with Peter was an easy decision but not one I took lightly. He was still finalizing his divorce, so we moved slowly. I didn't want to add to the confusion the girls must have felt. Meeting Grace inspired me with confidence somehow. I had expected some resistance, some reservation, being Peter's first relationship and being divorced myself. But Grace never hesitated with me. She had been my unexpected safety net as I tightroped my way into the family. She steadied us all and never seemed affected by the family's contortions. I wondered now if perhaps my own sense of imbalance at that time had prevented me from seeing any evidence of chaos in Grace. Even asking this question unsettled me. Surely if Grace had been experiencing Alzheimer's symptoms, I would, should have, seen some trace? The question gnawed at me. Perhaps I had been too busy trying to keep myself balanced that I missed the quiver in Grace's footfalls.

Dr. Gaede's words ran through my head, his explanation that we were seeing now the symptoms of a problem that had begun years ago. A disease that progressed in fits and starts, lying in wait before spawning a flurry of changes. I knew that evidence of the disease was woven through my memories, whether I could find those threads or not. The lure of hindsight promised to reveal what I had not seen the first time. And where did that leave me? What did it matter where the starting line was in this race Grace was running? What would hindsight achieve but blame and distraction? It occurred to me that maybe it was better that I couldn't find the disease in these early memories. What would finding such evidence do but add to my own sense of having failed Grace? Could it even undermine the confidence that she had given me in the last ten years?

I stepped back, out of the past, leaving my earliest memories of Grace intact. There was no value in tainting them with questions and recriminations that could never be assuaged. Hindsight was a fool's errand, and I was not going to be a fool. I was not going to move forward into the next stage with Grace with my eyes trained on the past, searching for blame. Grace deserved better than that. She was still strong now, but her memories were going to fade and she would one day become confusion itself. On that day, she would greet me with a genuine smile and hold my hand in hers even though she would be unable to pull my name from under her hat. And on that day, I would need my memories of her to hold close, memories untainted by hindsight's callous stare.

Chapter Three

The Gift of Insight

Insight comes with experience and with practice, letting us see past confusion to find logic in chaos. There are times when insight, and the confidence that it brings, is welcome. Sometimes insight makes us brave. But there are other times when insight reveals ugly truths, creates new panic, new confusion. In those moments, insight feels like a burden that makes it hard to move forward. So insight is a double-edged sword.

"It's better once you know," I've been told. "It makes things easier." I've said these things to myself, trying to counter bad news with the hope that preparation will make things easier to bear. But I'm not sure I believe these words. Sometimes, knowing is a distraction, a blindfold that makes all the familiar things in my life feel foreign. There have been times when I've traded naive hope for understanding and realized only after the exchange was made that I'd lost something valuable. Hope is a prize that can be difficult to reclaim. And yet I reach for insight because it feels like the right thing to do. Because it feels like the safest way to proceed in the darkness of Alzheimer's disease.

Sometimes, though, insight is a reward. There have been times when I've expected loss and found gain. Not all changes are bad; not all needs signal a deficit. Sometimes I look carefully, only to discover that I've ceded too much to this disease, that I've let go too early. Then insight lets me reclaim parts of Grace that I thought were gone. Sometimes my insight into Grace and her disease teaches me about myself, and in those moments, I am rewarded for the risk of wondering, of wanting to understand. Insight helps to map my new world, making it possible to navigate. It doesn't matter what the map looks like. It matters that I am with Grace, trying to understand our route, trying to keep our bearings in the confusion.

***

The morning after the diagnosis, I lay awake in my bed, confused at what I was supposed to do now that I knew that Grace had Alzheimer's disease. I had been living with the uncertainty for months; now it was a certainty.

I knew when I booked the appointment that there was something shifting in Grace, something that might prove significant. I refused to speculate on what Dr. Gaede might say because I couldn't imagine a scenario where his words wouldn't change our lives in some fundamental way. I had spent my energy holding my concerns at bay until that day came. I had saved enough mental energy to hear Dr. Gaede say "Alzheimer's disease" and then smile calmly at Grace as we left his office. That was the extent of my preparation for this diagnosis. I'd told myself that I could do nothing until I knew what I was facing, assuming that my sense of helplessness stemmed from my confusion, from my lack of knowledge. I expected that Grace's diagnosis would provide me with a map; I expected that knowing the disease's name would help me to find my way through the strange terrain Grace had been wandering through.

When I woke up in Palm Desert, on the first day after meeting with Dr. Gaede, I reached immediately for the diagnosis in my mind, like some people might reach for a cigarette or glance at a clock. I held the diagnosis for a moment, relieved to be holding something solid, no longer clinging to wispy possibilities. But as I lay there, repeating the word to myself, the feeling of relief began to drop away, and slowly and steadily, panic took its place. The words *Alzheimer's disease* were ugly. Foreign. Dangerous. These words didn't give me confidence; it felt impossible to rescue Grace from this reality. I searched my mind for connections to this disease and found images of old men and women straining to grasp escaped ideas, brows furrowed, eyes averted. I saw silent people, hollow and alone, people turned inward. I heard nothing. No questions, no laughter. I saw loneliness imposed from the inside. I felt hurt creeping through me as I looked into these faces, hurt that began to rattle in me until it was panic, full-blown. Panic at the thought that Grace could disappear like that. Would disappear like that. From here, I imagined Grace's future. I imagined my way through months and years, watching the disease age and steal her until I could see her clearly among the other patients in my mind, a bone china woman, her mouth moving silently, her eyes a perfect, empty blue. I realized I was letting my imagination get ahead of me. The vision ended abruptly then, fading away as a cold tight sweat across my chest.

I instinctively wrapped my arms around myself and buried my head under the blankets, not wanting Grace to hear me cry. If she heard me, she'd knock gently on the door and then ease into the room, her tone soothing. She would smooth back my hair and rub the heel of her hand across my back like I was one of her own children. And while I badly wanted reassurance this morning, I couldn't face being comforted by Grace. It was Grace's future I was mourning and my own. I couldn't share my fears with her; I couldn't explain what I was crying for. And I couldn't help but remind myself that there would be a time when she wouldn't be able to comfort me, when she wouldn't remember my name or why I smiled when she walked into the room. One day, she wouldn't have the instinct to reach out to me. This idea haunted me while I began to cry again, and eventually I just gave in, no longer restraining all the horrors I had been so afraid to examine before the appointment. I saw Grace grow listless and peevish; I saw her grow angry and mean. I watched her turn away from Peter, disinterested. I imagined finding her silent in a chair, her eyes vacant and her mouth hanging open, unreachable, and I saw myself knocked breathless by my fear that she wouldn't return to me. Under the thick white duvet, I conjured my worst fears, terrified by the knowledge that one day, I would discover that they had all come true.

I cried for a long time, giving in to all the worry that had been strapped across my chest for months. I felt myself surrendering to the fears I'd been ignoring for so long. My heart felt this diagnosis as a trauma, but a pragmatic voice in me started to whisper, asking me practical questions, reminding me that my tears were no solution. I cried for, and in spite of, these voices until I was finally exhausted. Visions of that silent, unsmiling Grace faded as I felt myself pulled back into the present. I mopped my eyes and lay still, enjoying my fatigue for the calm that it brought me. Minutes later, the heat of the blanket compelled me to throw the covers back. The bright sun streamed through the window next to the bed, and I squinted around the room, reassured by the familiarity. It seemed genuinely strange to me that nothing had changed, that the diagnosis hadn't had a physical impact on the room, on the house. "Nothing's different, I guess," I muttered as I swung my legs off the bed, feeling for my slippers.

Sitting on the edge of the mattress, I turned to look at the other side of the bed, which was empty. Peter was in Calgary. We had planned that I would take Grace to the appointment with Dr. Gaede. The appointment would have felt too significant if Peter had been there. I was used to managing situations alone, but getting married was beginning to change that. Peter and I talked strategy together and faced situations with a united front—Bob's cancer and Peter's brother Rob's addiction to alcohol and drugs. But I didn't want to add Grace to that list until it was absolutely necessary. Thinking about it now, I could see that I had been minimizing the significance of the appointment, wanting to see it as something I could handle alone. Because I'd been handling things alone my whole life, I wanted to feel I could handle this as well. In truth, I had half-convinced myself I would return home with no diagnosis at all. I'd wanted everything to be okay, and I hadn't really prepared myself for anything else. I wasn't prepared to accept this diagnosis, and I wasn't prepared to talk about it either.

Grace could always sense when people were fragile. Whenever she felt tension or hurt in a person, she'd curl up beside them like a cat settling into a lap, chatting in low tones like a steady purr. For those few days in Palm Desert, Grace stayed close to me, wanting me to feel wordlessly supported, and I could see concern in her eyes. I toyed with the words for a long time before I explained to her, haltingly, that I had just found out that one of my girlfriends was sick and that I didn't know how to help her. Grace didn't ask for details; she didn't need them. She could understand my sense of helplessness. More importantly, she knew how much I hated feeling unsure of myself. After a long hug, she leaned back on the couch with me and in a calm, motherly voice, she asked, "How are you going to handle this?" I demurred, not sure of how to respond, but she let me sit quietly and then asked again what I thought I should do. And so I talked to Grace, carefully, about my friend, about how I wished I could do something to help her. Grace smiled and told me that all I needed to do was be available, to be a support. She held my hand as we talked, and the tone of her voice soothed me, helping me to see past the diagnosis that was unnerving me. And somewhere along the way, I realized that I was so fixated on Grace's future that I was forgetting the present, where Grace was still with me, helping me. There would be so much time to battle the disease; why was I letting the fight start now? Why was I mourning Grace rather than embracing this woman beside me?

Later, after Grace and I had dinner and then settled in the living room with books, I let my thoughts turn to the future and how this reality would play out. Peter and I had recently been sketching out plans for the time after Katie, our youngest daughter, graduated from university. We hadn't been rushing toward it, but we had begun laying down provisional plans for our free time after she left the nest. Peter was an adventurer at heart, and recently he'd been writing me in as an enthusiastic partner in his travels. I wanted to see life in other places; I wanted to sit in foreign cafes and order elaborate dishes in the local language.

It had become a bit of a game between us, batting destinations and experiences at each other like shuttlecocks. "Let's sail down through the Caribbean," Peter would offer as I walked through the bedroom door. I'd stop and take up a thinking pose. "How about tapas on Crete?" I'd offer back, and he'd assume my same pose and we'd both laugh. We hadn't settled on anything specific, but it felt exciting to imagine fewer responsibilities and more freedom to explore.

I was starting to realize in the wake of the diagnosis that neither of us had really factored in the possibility that Grace would need us at home. She'd taken Bob's death in stride; nursing him in the later stages of his cancer seemed to prepare her for life without him. Of course, the fact that in Calgary we lived just around the corner made it easy for us to help her adjust to being on her own. Bob had been a take-charge man, and he had sheltered Grace from practical decisions, so we worried that she would be adrift without him. But when we would compare notes about how Grace seemed, Peter always sounded a positive note. In part, I think Peter didn't like to think of his mother as a frail widow, but he was also right about Grace. She had wrangled a good deal of independence from Bob without ever challenging him; she was shrewdly aware of the balance she needed to strike. Peter had a collection of anecdotes about Grace, all of which highlighted her capability, and he pulled them out while the rest of us worried. His favorite by far was about "Presenting Italy."

This story had been told and retold within the family for years. One afternoon, Peter and I and Pamela and her husband sat in the kitchen, trading notes about Grace's conduct since Bob's death, while Grace rested. Peter interjected, "She's not helpless. She's not. She might have seemed that way with dad, but that's just the roles they fell into." He paused, seeing both his parents in his mind, and then he launched into his story and his eyes lit up at the memory of Grace in her element. "I don't know where she got the idea, really. I mean, it's one thing to have a good eye for design, it's another to open your own store. Can you imagine," he said, gesturing specifically at Pamela, "how brave Mom was to sit down with Grandfather and explain that she wanted a loan to finance a boutique? He probably stopped her at the word *boutique*, just stopped her and said, 'Sorry, Grace, that doesn't sound like a good investment.' But she explained her business plans and inventory sources and answered every question he asked until he agreed to loan her the money. He had such a soft spot for her. That's Mom," he said almost fiercely. "That's the woman she is." Peter shook his head, smiling. There was a pause as Peter's vision of Grace stood in the room with us. I'd seen pictures of her at the shop, always bright-eyed and beautiful. I understood why Peter loved this memory of her most of all.

His voice was full of pride, and he sat back and started to paint the image in his head for the rest of us, using his hands for emphasis. "She succeeded against all odds. It opened on the top floor of a three-story building without an elevator. Yet on that first day, there was a crowd of people there to watch her cut the ribbon. She stepped forward to say a few words, and then stood back and pointed to the store sign and said 'Presenting Italy!'"

This memory wasn't Peter's; I knew that. He was twenty-five when Grace opened the store, in the midst of sailing around the world, and he missed the ribbon cutting. But there were photos from the day, of Grace and Bob and Frank, Bob's dad, who had loaned Grace the money she needed to open the store in the first place. I'd seen those pictures and heard Peter's retelling often enough to feel that I had been there as well. "She loved that store—she loved everything about it. She chose everything herself. 'We carry only the very best, Peter,' she used to say to me. 'I only choose the best.'" Peter paused as he always did when he told this part of the story, and we all smiled at the image of Grace in our heads. Bob's voice popped into my head then, as if he was in the room with us: "Grace's little hobby." That's what he always said about Presenting Italy even when it became the most fashionable boutique women's clothing store in Calgary, even when she sold the store at a massive profit. "Grace's little hobby." But I didn't want to sidetrack the memory conjured in the kitchen, so I said nothing.

Pamela piped up, eager to add to the nostalgia and the pride. "Do you remember when she would take those trips to Europe for clothes? And when she came back from one trip, one early trip, she had boxes and boxes, and when she brought us to the store to see, it was all antiques, chandeliers, and artisan stuff! Barely a dress in sight! I thought she was crazy, but she just laughed and shook her head, saying, 'I am in the business of selling the best. I might have been looking for clothes, but a treasure is a treasure!' And she was right, everything sold. She always had such a sense of taste. And she knew most of her customers by name. She made everyone feel so welcome. When someone would come through the door, their eyes would light up and they would run right toward her and chat before they looked at anything. And then Mom would lead them around the store, picking out things that would suit them. And she'd always be able to remember where she found each piece, and tell that story too. It's a wonder she got anyone to leave!"

There was a small silence as Pamela's husband pressed his hand across Pamela's shoulder, and then she sighed. "You're right, Peter. Maybe I overestimate how dependent she was on Dad to get by but she's held everything together well enough. Presenting Italy was something she did entirely on her own. Mom won't go to pieces without Dad." And for a minute, we all thought about this disparity between Grace the wife and Grace the entrepreneur. I liked this particular story about Grace because I could understand how important that business was to her and how she must have worked to balance her life so that no one felt neglected. It made me feel akin to her somehow, knowing that we'd both needed to create something of our own, something that shaped us and thrilled us. I said none of this, but it was a thought that lifted me up and worried me as I was about Grace's adjustment to being on her own.

We talked late into the night, about Bob and about Grace, about everything. Peter and Pamela held court, telling stories from their childhood, painting Bob and Grace anew for their rapt audience. It was good to laugh with the pleasure of our memories. We agreed it would be best to let Grace tell us what she needed instead of trying to push our plans on her. The fact that we lived so close to them in Calgary made it easy to agree to this approach. Peter and I would have her over for dinner a few nights a week, and we'd drop in on her casually the rest of the time to make sure that she was managing everything herself. It would have happened like this even if we hadn't sat down to discuss it; Peter and I had gotten used to Grace and Bob popping in and out of our lives since moving close to them. Grace helped us get over Bob's death as much as we helped her live without him. For the first few weeks, settling down together felt a little strange; Bob was always center stage, telling jokes, filling the room with his presence. Our gatherings felt a little small without him, but slowly, we found new routines and started to relax into them. Grace became a little more vocal and held the floor a little longer than she used to. I sometimes wondered if she was trying, in her small way, to cover over Bob's absence for our sakes.

Having Grace with us so often made my life easier and better. She became a steadying force in my day, and I looked forward to chatting things over with her on the nights when we ate dinner together. I remember laughing when friends of mine groaned for me, living with my solitary mother-in-law just down the road and at my dinner table every other night; I could never convince them that Grace wasn't like any mother-in-law I'd ever known. "We're friends, honestly. She's like a mom without any of the complicated politics but with all the love and support. She's amazing—it's so easy." The stories my friends would tell about their husbands' mothers seemed a world apart from my friendship with Grace, and I could do nothing but shake my head and listen, privately counting my blessings.

But sitting on the couch with Grace after her diagnosis, it was hard to recover the confidence I felt for her after Bob's death. It was impossible to recall the breezy tone I used when talking to friends about her. This disease didn't care how wonderful she was. There was no treatment; there was no chance of recovery. That thought was terrifying. Mixed into my depression was rage: rage that Grace wouldn't get the chance to fight this disease, to test her mettle against it like the other challenges in her life. If surviving this diagnosis was a matter of will, I would have felt determination, conviction, confidence. I would put my money on Grace every day of the week. But this diagnosis didn't even give her the chance to fight. Suddenly, seeing her as an Alzheimer's disease patient, Grace's future seemed dark to me, and it would always be getting darker. The longer she lived, the longer that I had her with me, the stronger the disease would get. And that seemed so unkind.

What made this worse was the fact that I wasn't able to talk this over with Grace; I had gotten used to having her as a sounding board for problems big and small, and now, facing the most frightening challenge of my life and hers, I felt that I couldn't say anything. Nor did I know what I should say to her or what she would say to me if I did confess what I had learned.

I hadn't ever expected that it would be easy to talk to Grace about the doctor's diagnosis, but now I found it impossible. I thought I had prepared myself for anything, even Alzheimer's disease, but hearing the words come out of Dr. Gaede's mouth, I felt something in me collapse. Why hadn't I prepared more for this news? And now that I knew, now that I knew that Grace was facing a worst-case scenario, what do I do with that knowledge?

***

Grace had once heard Peter say the words *Alzheimer's disease*; it was months and months ago, but I still remembered it. I had walked over to pick up Grace for dinner and she answered the door, beaming when she saw me. "Hi, Grace," I said brightly, leaning in to kiss her cheek. "I thought I'd escort you to dinner. Peter's in charge in the kitchen tonight." I expected Grace to usher me into the condo but her feet didn't step back.

When I looked up, her face was stern, with a line of worry dotted across her forehead. "I'm not eating with you and Peter tonight. I'm eating here—no one talked to me about eating with you." Her words were neutral, but her tone wasn't. Her voice was tight and strained. Like she felt she was being pushed in some undesirable direction.

"Didn't Peter call you yesterday?" I asked, frustrated that he must have forgotten. "I'm sorry, Grace—Peter must have been confused. You know how busy he is at work. He must have assumed you would be free and forgot to check." I smiled at her, expecting her to nod and shake her head at Peter's mistake.

But she didn't nod. "No one told me about dinner," she insisted again. Her tone was unfamiliar; Grace was usually very accommodating, so it was strange to find her inflexible over something as small as dinner. I apologized again, shaking my head at Peter's error, anxious to let the matter drop. Grace went to get her purse, and when she returned, she seemed to have forgotten her frustration, so I smiled and escorted her out the door.

Later, while Grace was still at the table, I cornered Peter in the kitchen, elbowing him gently in the ribs. "Hey, you said you called your mom yesterday about dinner."

Peter set down his handful of glasses and turned toward me easily. "Yeah," he said, smiling.

I continued. "Grace was surprised when I got over there. She said you didn't call." I tried to keep my voice neutral, not sure of the right tone for this conversation. I didn't want to blow this out of proportion, but I didn't want to miss something either. "Are you sure that you called? And that you were clear about the date and time?"

Peter nodded. "I called yesterday. And doesn't she come here every Tuesday? It's not like it's unusual for her to be here tonight."

I cringed inwardly, knowingly stepping into dangerous terrain. "Her memory loss is starting to concern me but I don't know if it's serious. It's hard to tell what's normal—she's eighty-two years old." I paused for a moment, considering my words before I spoke again. "There are a lot of causes of memory loss, and some are treatable and some . . . aren't." Peter looked away, not just away from me but far away. The whole house was quiet, seeming to wait for him to speak again. I spoke first. "Peter, this is just a conversation. We are probably jumping to conclusions. Grace is getting older. It makes sense that her memory would get a little . . . inaccurate." He nodded, and swallowed, wary of the implications of our discussion. I wished in the moment that I hadn't brought it up at all.

He breathed in deeply, "It could be something serious, though, right? It could be something like Alzheimer's dis—" The words didn't make it out of his mouth, and for a split second, I assumed that the thought was too upsetting to voice.

Then I heard the brittle noise of plates being placed on the counter and knew that Grace was behind me. When I turned, Grace was standing ready, indignation gripping her face. "How dare you, Peter! I do not have that disease!" She was angry to have been accused like this, but she didn't stare Peter and I down the way I expected she would from her initial response. There was a tiny quiver in her voice that told me that she was unnerved by what we had said, and she looked at each of us and then away as if she was trying to compose herself. And then again, she spoke. "I don't have that disease. I don't!"

I spoke up, ready to retract it all, feeling this was my error. "Grace, I'm so sorry. I shouldn't have said anything. I was out of line. I'm sorry."

Peter murmured an apology as well, and after a tense silence, Grace relented, still holding herself stiffly. "That's okay," she said, turning back to the dining room to finish clearing the table. I glanced at Peter, feeling chastened. We all worked quietly to clean up the kitchen, and I tried to cover the silence with chatter, hoping to distract Grace from her hurt long enough for her better nature to properly forgive us. By the time we walked her home that night, she seemed to have let the matter drop.

And so we tucked the event away, not wanting to read too much into it. Had we known more, we might have realized that more significant than the forgetting was Grace's reaction to the words *Alzheimer's disease*. Her response was out of character. But we didn't know what to look for. We didn't realize the quiet battle she must have been having with her own fears. Like almost anyone her age, she had friends who had fallen victim to this disease. As she found herself forgetting things more often, the visions of those friends must have haunted her. Like most Alzheimer's disease patients, however, she fought to keep anyone from suspecting what was happening.

From that night on, Peter and I watched Grace more carefully. We watched her for almost a year before we decided that we needed to consult a doctor, until we were able to point to undeniable changes in her behavior. I didn't like doing it, because it felt disingenuous. Grace and I were close, and it was against my instinct to keep things from her; I worried over how she would react if she got the sense that we were evaluating her. She had revealed her hand, that night in the kitchen when she reacted so badly to the words Alzheimer's disease. Whether she could see it herself or not, there was something there.

I hated to admit it but it seemed that, as soon as we resolved to start watching Grace more closely, we started to notice things. Mostly, they were simple things that I might have done myself, things I would have laughed at and waved off. But somehow, after Grace's strong reaction, they seemed to point to some shift in her.

One of the most disconcerting things we noticed had to do with Grace's driving. She had a little car for tooling around and getting groceries, and as she had her eyes checked once a year, we didn't give a thought to it. That changed one Sunday afternoon. We were expecting Grace for dinner. She said she would be over after running some errands. At three that afternoon, Peter popped his head into the living room and asked if Grace had called. "She's doing errands, so I think it's a loose deadline today," I replied, looking up from my book.

Peter paused before he replied, "I just thought she would be finished by now—she was only going to the grocery store, and she lives alone—it's never a big purchase." He drummed his fingers along the wall, and the noise caught my attention. Peter did not linger. It wasn't conversation that was holding him here, so it must have been something else. It must have been Grace.

I put down the book, folding it closed on my lap, and looked up at him. "Peter, are you worried? I'm sure she's fine—she probably stopped in somewhere to get a dessert for dinner. You know she loves bringing something nice. Or she had something else to do that she didn't mention. She's still your mother. She doesn't tell you everything." I laughed a little but quietly; I could see that my words were not having much of an effect on him. "Have you tried calling her?" I offered.

"Yes, I called, but it goes to voicemail. She's not there," Peter replied. For a second, I thought that there might be something really wrong, but then I pulled back. She hadn't set a time to come over, and she had said she was going out. There was nothing to get nervous about.

Checking my watch, I considered the time and then looked back at Peter. "Let's give it an hour, and then we can walk over to her condo, okay? I don't want her thinking that we're checking up on her."

Peter considered and then looked at his watch again. "Fine, four o'clock, then I'm going over," he said and headed off down the hallway. I could tell from the way he left that he was still worried. I sat, thinking over the situation for a minute. Was Peter too concerned? Was I too relaxed? There was no right answer.

Grace called the house just before four. Peter answered and I could hear him asking about her afternoon, not wanting to confess his worry to her. After a minute, I heard him telling her about dinner—about his marinated steaks—and I relaxed. We were nervous, and nervous people find a lot to be afraid of. I turned back to my book, only to have Peter walk into the room, still holding the phone. "She said she went to the grocery store at 2:00 p.m.," he started. I nodded, waiting for his larger point. "And she said she just got home now, just now," he said.

"So she took a long time at the grocery store, or maybe she didn't pay attention to the time that she left. She's safe now, and that's all that matters, right? In the long run?" I asked, not sure where the conversation was going.

Peter sighed a little and moved to sit beside me on the couch. "I know I'm making a big deal out of this, but it's just a little weird, and we are supposed to be watching for weird right now. I commented that it was a long trip, and she said that Sixteenth Avenue was blocked off and she had to circle around to get home."

I mentally mapped the route to the grocery store and queried, "That's nowhere near the store. Did she say why she was up there?"

Peter sighed again. "No, she said she went straight to the store and back."

The feeling in the room was suddenly tense, or maybe I was just starting to feel the tension that Peter had been holding on to for the last hour. I mentally ran through a trip to the grocery store and acknowledged the strangeness of the situation to Peter. "Two hours to go to the store doesn't make sense. It's five minutes away. And Grace has lived here for years. She knows the area better than we do." I felt frustrated that I had no answer, that I couldn't just ask Grace about what had happened. Having no options made me want to push the whole issue away. "This is weird. I'm not going to say it isn't. But what do we have to go on right now? She must have gotten the time wrong." Again, there was nothing solid we could point to, and so we resolved to just keep watching, waiting for some proof that there was a real problem.

The first real proof came when Grace's sister Colleen in Phoenix arrived to visit Grace in Calgary. The two of them had the whole week planned out, and from what I heard from Grace, everything was going well, so I was surprised when Colleen pulled me aside one evening just before dinner, leaving Grace with Peter in the living room. As she eased in beside me, I turned and smiled. "Colleen! Have you been having a good time out here? Have you two girls been getting into trouble?" I started to laugh, but Colleen's face got cloudy. "Are you okay, Colleen? Is everything okay? I was only teasing!" I offered.

Colleen looked away. "It's about Grace," Colleen began, looking over her shoulder toward the living room. I felt my heart drop. I had said to myself that, if anyone would spot trouble with Grace, it was Colleen.

I cleared my throat. "Of course, Colleen, what is it?" I asked, trying to keep my tone even.

"Well, we . . . we went out this afternoon to see a matinee, and we drove there, and that part was fine. But when we got back to the car, Grace just sat there. She put the key in the ignition and turned the car on, but that's it. And when I asked her what she was waiting for, she said she was thinking about what the best way home was." I felt my jaw clench but said nothing, and Colleen continued. "Well, I said we should just go the way we came, but Grace didn't respond. She just kept looking out the window, so I sat. I kept thinking, 'How long could she want to sit for?' but she just kept sitting. And when I started to talk again, she snapped at me and said, 'How am I supposed to think with you asking questions!'"

Colleen looked into the living room at Grace, who was listening to Peter relay some story about work. "So how did you get home then?" I asked.

"Oh, well, after all the waiting, Grace turned to me and said, 'Home?' and I said yes, and she started to drive. I don't know what route she took, but it was much longer than the route we took to get to the theater. I kept looking for Macleod Trail—that's the only street I know that's close to your house—but I never saw it. And she was quiet the whole way home. Like she was really concentrating on where she was. I tried to commiserate and tell her how confusing some of the roads in Phoenix are, but she wouldn't listen at all. She just kept snapping at me. When we got home, I dropped it and she's been fine since." There was a pause. Colleen seemed deflated after telling her story and a little out of breath. It was a shared sentiment. I could imagine Grace driving around, confused about where she was. It clicked that that must have been the delay weeks ago. She must have gotten lost and just driven until she found her way again. The idea of that . . . I couldn't think about it.

I took Colleen's hands in my own. "I'm so sorry, Colleen. We've been watching Grace for signs that she is having problems with her memory but we've never seen anything definitive, and the only time we mentioned it in front of her, she got really defensive. We had no idea that she was having serious trouble. You must have been so worried, driving along and not able to say anything to her," I offered.

Colleen must have heard the worry in my voice because her brows lifted as she responded, "Really, it's fine—a senior moment, I think, and she didn't want to admit it to me. Maybe she thought I'd tease her about my being younger!" Colleen responded, smiling ruefully. "You know Grace—quietly determined!" I nodded, and I could feel myself relax a little. I knew it was the term *senior moment*; it took the edge off of Colleen's story. Maybe Colleen was right; Grace was getting older. Maybe we left her with too much responsibility. She hated to be a burden. Maybe she didn't want us to know she was having problems. Maybe she felt embarrassed. That was understandable. In those few moments, I resolved it in my mind. Grace was getting older; she needed more help.

I gave Colleen a quick hug and smiled at her. "Thanks, Colleen—we'll keep a closer eye on her. She doesn't tend to do a lot of driving anyway, so Peter and I can easily offer to go with her," I said.

Colleen smiled brightly at me. "Well, she's in good hands!" she said and turned back toward the living room, where Grace was rooting through a drawer, looking for a pack of cards.

"Rummy?" she called loudly, looking at us in the kitchen.

Colleen responded, "Yes, yes," and started to move to the door, where she paused and looked back at me. "Don't worry too much, it happens to us all. You can see yourself that she's fine." And when we looked back, Grace was dealing the cards into two neat piles on the coffee table. And like that, the conversation was dropped.

But not for long. Peter returned home one day after riding along to the mall with Grace. I could tell from his demeanor that he was concerned and wanted to talk. "She got us to the mall okay. She parked the car and went into one of the mall entrances. It was a busy day so there were a lot of cars in the lot," he said. "When we were done shopping, I could tell she was unsure about which exit to use. I got us to the right exit but then decided to try a test. I wasn't trying to be mean," he explained. "I just wanted to what she would do. When she asked where the car was parked, I pretended that I hadn't been paying attention. I could see a little look of panic in her expression though she tried not to show it. 'I think it's this way,' she said and headed off the wrong way down one of the aisles. I didn't let her wander too long before

I said, 'No, I think it is over this way.'" I heard the sadness and concern in Peter's voice. "Honestly, Connie, she wasn't even close. I don't know what she would have done if she had been alone. What does she do when she is on her own and forgets like that . . . just wander up and down all the aisles until she finds her car?" There was no easy answer to that question but I felt I needed to find one.

The next morning, I did a search on the Internet for "memory loss seniors." Some of the results I could rule out right away, like drug use or medications. But others jumped out at me: nutritional deficiency, thyroid problems, and depression. All these could be the cause. I tried not to focus on the worst options: stroke and Alzheimer's disease. They were serious problems, and there was just no evidence of either of them. I focused on depression because it seemed the most likely and the easiest to handle. Grace had had her thyroid removed year ago, so it couldn't be that. Of course, the idea that Grace was depressed and hadn't said anything was unsettling. My research said that it was essential to talk with a doctor if there were clear indications or symptoms. But again, I wondered if maybe it was just aging. Peter and I resolved to minimize her time in the car and watch her carefully. If there was anything strange, we'd act.

I suggested to Grace that she and I start doing groceries together, and she was happy to do so. I made it a regular event on Saturdays, and when we had unpacked everything in both our kitchens, we would have fruit and cheese for lunch. For weeks, our new routine gave Peter and me a sense of calm. Grace seemed completely fine. One Saturday, as we were standing in the checkout line, Grace started a little and looked up at me. "Soya sauce," she said.

I cocked my head, wondering what she meant, and leaned toward her as if I hadn't heard her correctly. "What was that, Grace?" I asked.

She waved a finger in my direction and smiled. "We forgot soya sauce. You said you needed some before we left your house, remember?" And thinking back to earlier, I did remember. I had said it more to myself than to Grace while I was running through a mental inventory of what we needed to buy. Grace had been at the door, getting her shopping bags and her purse together; I hadn't realized that she was listening.

And standing in the line, I leaned toward her and wrapped my arms around her, nearly ready to cry. "What would I do without you, Grace?" I asked.

She laughed gently and pulled away from me so that I could see her face. "Well, if I'm going to do the remembering, you better do the running," she exclaimed and moved out of the way so that I could go back to the aisles. "I'll buy my things first, and by the time you get back, it will be your turn," she said.

I took a deep breath and nodded. "Great, I'll be right back, Grace," I said, walking toward the aisles, wanting to skip. Wanting to sing. It was an overreaction, I know, but it felt so good to have some positive evidence instead of a confirmation of the fears that Peter and I didn't want to discuss.

When we got home, I told the story to Peter as Grace and I unpacked my bags, looking at him significantly when I held up the bottle of soya sauce. He laughed and clapped Grace gently on the back before leaning in toward her. "It's good that you were with her, Mom. Connie can be ve-ry for-get-ful!" Grace waved his words away and defended me as I knew she would. She was always everybody's champion.

Then only a few days later, the pendulum swung the other way, hard and fast. I had taken the day off so that I could drop my car by a garage and had planned to spend the day with Grace. She was going to follow me to the mechanic in her car, and then we were going to go to the Glenbow Museum followed by lunch at the Calgary Tower. The restaurant had huge floor-to-ceiling windows and revolved ever so slightly during the meal so that we could see the whole city. I drove to Grace's and found her already in her car in the parking lot. I waved and then turned around, and we set off, a tiny little convoy of two. I drove slowly to make sure that we didn't get separated, watching her in the rearview mirror. It wasn't far, and when we arrived, she parked along the street while I went in to drop off my keys. When I came back out, she had turned the car around and was ready to go, so I slid in beside her. "Are you ready for our adventure?" she asked, smiling at me, and I nodded and held one arm out, gesturing toward the road.

It was only a few minutes to the museum, and traffic was light, so I relaxed into the seat. As we rolled toward the first red light at a fairly quick speed, I instinctively pushed my right foot into the floor, willing the car to slow down. And after a second, the car did start to slow down, although I found my back pressed into the car seat as we got closer to the line of cars. Once we were stopped at the light, I relaxed again, wilfully. We eased along in traffic slowly so that a space grew between our car and the car in front of us, and even when Grace got up to speed, she didn't close that gap. "Still," I told myself, "better slow than fast." And then the sentence repeated in my mind, and I remembered Peter telling me that slow drivers often cause accidents. At each light, I had the same sense that she wasn't noticing the light and that we were braking late, that we might not stop in time. My foot was pressed to the floor in sympathy with my instinct to slow Grace down, but even though she ended up braking hard, she never rolled past the line, so I said nothing. At least until the next corner.

She pulled into the turning lane on Tenth Avenue without turning on her signal. When the light changed, she rolled off the line, driving straight ahead before making an awkward arc that landed her on the extreme far side of the road. My shoulder was pressed against the glass of the window for a long moment, and I felt my body weight notably shift in my seat. I didn't hesitate. "Ooh, Grace, that was a sharp turn!"

Grace looked up at me, surprised. "I'm sorry, Connie. It didn't feel sharp to me." Her concern seemed to distract her, so I waved her eyes back to the road.

We were on a four-lane road with synchronized lights. Midmorning, the road was half-full, and Grace was sliding through each light. And picking up speed. Traffic was moving just at the speed limit, and Grace was definitely moving a bit faster. This was not the same woman who had crept along so carefully just five minutes ago. Now Grace was bright, animated in her driving, and as we moved along, we caught up to the car in front of us. I expected her to slow down, to settle into the lane and cruise, but instead she kept her pace and veered left into the next lane. Seeing cars in front of her in that lane as well, she yanked the wheel again and landed in the second of the four lanes. Her eyes never looked anywhere but forward. There was a honk behind her, loud enough to grab my attention, but Grace ignored it.

My hands were pressed along the side of my chair, and I was sitting up, straight up, with my body tight. "Could you slow down a little, Grace," I asked in a strained voice. "I'm feeling a little off."

Grace looked at me with concern, but I shooed her eyes back to the road. "Not far now, Connie," Grace offered, slowing down in the lane.

For three blocks, Grace's car moved with the others at an even pace, then I saw Grace's head duck, looking forward and up along the buildings. "What's the cross-street, Connie?" she asked, still scanning. Looking back at the road, I saw that Grace had been so busy looking for the turn, she had drifted right, sailing down the road in two lanes instead of one.

"Over, over, over!" I shouted, and Grace snapped her eyes back on the road, pulling on the wheel.

"Sorry!" she said, easing back off the pedal. I breathed heavily, and steeled myself.

What was this? I thought as we finally pulled into the parking lot. What the hell was this? When was the last time we had driven together in her car? She had driven me to the grocery store not long ago, and her driving had been slow and plodding. When was the last time we had been on a big road in traffic? That was harder to answer. We tended to take my car when we went shopping together. But this . . . this was serious. She wasn't safe driving like this. I needed to talk to Peter before I did anything else.

When I described my experience to Peter, his reaction was immediate. "Connie, this is serious. I noticed a few new dings and bumps on her car last week but I didn't think much about it then. If this is how she's driving, we have to do something drastic. We need to take away her car keys before it's too late and someone gets hurt." I felt my face go slack as I remembered what Grace's sister had said about Grace's confusion and considered it alongside what I had seen today. Peter was right: we couldn't let Grace keep driving. It just wasn't safe.

I found myself blinking back tears. They were tears of confusion, spurred by my fear of confronting Grace, of undermining her, and my frustration that she had suddenly become old. I didn't resent the need to care for her, but I was angry that I was becoming the person who took away Grace's freedoms and pleasures. Grace and I were friends; we had been friends since the first day we met, and I didn't want that dynamic to change. But how did I remain her friend while acting like her parent? I had no answer. Peter's eyebrows furrowed slightly the way they always did when he was puzzling over something. There was a brief silence, and then he spoke. "We have to be direct. She's not safe, and we have to make sure she's safe. She'll see that, don't you think?" I didn't think so, but I didn't want to undercut Peter's tentative confidence.

We had precedent on our side; Grace had friends whose kids had taken away the car keys for similar reasons. But I knew she was proud to still be driving after so many of her friends had lost their driving privileges. It would be one of those discussions where no matter how we phrased our concerns, Grace would hear "You are getting old. You need to be watched. You can't have your freedom anymore."

"We need to explain the problem and talk it over with her. Perhaps if she did poorly on an eye test, there might be less sting than us just saying 'We don't trust you anymore,'" I offered, feigning confidence. We talked about it for a long time, planning phrases that wouldn't ruffle feathers, practicing kindness in response to anger.

Peter booked two appointments with an eye doctor and called Grace to make sure she was free the next morning. Grace was surprised at the offer but agreed immediately. She loved going out with Peter; she loved saying "This is Peter, my son" with swelling pride in her voice. She liked walking with him, arm in arm. I've never had children of my own, but watching Grace with Peter, I could understand her parental pride. In part, it came from knowing that she had held his hands from his first minutes of life and had helped him to grow into a successful, happy man.

I left them to do the trip together, and when they got back to Grace's condo, I walked over. We had agreed on a loose plan for our conversation with Grace, but I felt anxious while they were out, knowing that Grace's pleasure at her errand with Peter would be cut short when she arrived home. I was relieved that Peter had decided to lead the conversation; we had agreed that it would seem less like judgment and more like concern if Peter raised the issue with Grace, starting with the eye test. We were about to encroach on her independence in a way that we had never done before, and putting myself in her place, I knew I would resist. Pamela and her husband were in agreement, but they were also safely down in Santa Fe, and Grace wouldn't blame them for this; she would blame us. She would fight us.

I focused on Peter's slow words. He started as we agreed that he should. "Mom, we need to talk to you about something really difficult." Grace looked up with evident concern, and then, a moment later, a shrewder expression passed across her face. She said nothing, waiting warily for Peter to continue. "It's about your driving." Peter paused, waiting for an objection, but Grace said nothing. She just stared at him with sharp disapproval, so he ventured forward again. "We don't feel it's safe for you to keep driving, Mom. Your eyesight isn't as good as it used to be." We had planned these words, planned to focus on the necessity of meeting legal requirements rather than suggesting there was some undefined problem with her.

Grace's eyes cut toward me and I had the instinct to look away, but the memory of the other day remained clear in my mind: I knew that she wasn't safe on the road anymore. This was difficult, but there was no way I could back down. This was not just about her safety but the safety of all the other drivers on the road. Grace's face fixed into a glare, her eyes narrowed and her shoulders hunched up, high and round. Her lips were tight and half-pursed, but she said nothing. I looked at Peter for direction, but he looked back at me, unsure. We had no real idea how to proceed.

I'd never started a conversation with Grace that felt so much like scolding. I waited for her to say something, but she sat unspeaking, clearly angry at us both. I caught Peter's eye and shrugged a little, wondering what would come next. We both turned back to Grace. After almost a minute of silence, I spoke again. "Do you want to say anything? Or do you want to think about this for a little while? I can see that you're—"

Grace's eyes cut toward me and, in a low voice, she spoke. "How would you feel? How would you feel if Lindsey did this to you?"

I felt myself deflate as I looked in her eyes and saw the cloud of emotions she was wrestling. It made no sense to lie to her, so I dropped my shoulders and answered honestly, "I'd be pissed, Grace." And it was clear that she was pissed, though she didn't try to argue with us. Instead, she was silent, her hands pulled in close to her chest, her lips pursed, her eyes averted. Peter and I kept up a discussion about how we would make sure she wasn't limited without the car, trying vainly to assure ourselves as well as Grace, but she refused to be engaged, and eventually, we gave up and said we would go home. Peter already had Grace's keys in his pocket; we had planned to take them with us. I leaned down to hug Grace, who was still in her chair, and she let me put my arms around her, although her body was stiff and her arms didn't reach around me. "Good-bye, Grace," I said gently. Peter hugged her as well and kissed her cheek, but she remained impassive and silent as we let ourselves out.

Grace's silence seemed to stay with us as we walked away, weighing our decision and trying to convince ourselves that we had handled the situation well. When we got home, I settled on the couch, but I could only think about Grace. Part of me felt that we had completed a herculean task, taking away Grace's keys. But part of me was still worried. We had solved the driving problem, but was there a darker problem just under the surface of the water? What else might be on the way for us, I wondered. I wasn't sure.

I made a point of calling Grace's friend, Ginia, a few days later. Ginia had moved to Calgary from Louisiana just before Grace had arrived from Virginia many years ago, and the two women bonded over their shared sense of dislocation during their first years in Canada. Determined to recreate a sense of community, they started a book club and, later, a supper club, which became a tradition that held them together for years and years. They raised their families together and celebrated as each child left the nest, and even now, they still saw each other regularly. She was one of the few friends Grace had who could still drive, and I wanted her to help me arrange rides for Grace when I couldn't get myself free from work. As soon as she heard my voice, hers softened, and I knew that she had already spoken to Grace. She asked how I was, and I tried to keep my voice light as I admitted that things had been better. She gave a low laugh and her ancient Southern accent warbled warmly over the phone: "I've been talking to Grace, Connie, all about you and Peter. She's really worked up over this car conversation. Do you know how angry she is?"

I took a quick breath, wanting to launch into an explanation of our reasons for taking the car, but realizing a moment later that it didn't matter. If Grace still needed to vent to Ginia, why try to take that away from her? Instead, I shook my head gently and a rueful smile slid across my face. "Yes, I know. But I can handle it." And once I'd said the words, I believed them. I could handle it. This was how things needed to be right now, and Grace would soften soon enough. Until then, I'd take the hit.

Ginia assured me that Grace's anger was burning out, that she would soon forget to be resentful, and promised to help me where she could with the driving. "It will give Grace and me an excuse to see more of each other, and it's no problem at all. Just let me know when you need me."

I felt relieved to have Ginia's support, and I hung up the phone, ready to reach out to Grace. I dialed her number, feeling a little nervous, and when she answered, there was a pause after I said hello where we both seemed to be struggling for the right words. I decided not to say anything at all about the car, wanting to leave it aside for a moment, and instead I told Grace about our dog Sasha, who had woken me up by barking hysterically at the squirrels that jumped from tree to tree in our small front yard. Grace's cool tone dropped away, distracted by the story, and when I finished, she said that she missed Sasha and asked if I was free to take a short walk, just the three of us. I smiled as I said yes, and promised to meet Grace halfway between our two homes. And so Grace began to forgive me.

For months after the removal of the car keys, we watched over Grace carefully while trying not to appear to be doing so. When we brought Grace down to Palm Desert for the winter, we arranged the calendar so that there was almost always somebody staying with her. Peter and I took the most shifts, but Pamela and Grace's sisters, Jean and Colleen, all took turns visiting Grace. Whatever else we told ourselves, it was clear that Grace wasn't completely capable anymore. There were other warning signs too: she'd lose her purse in her living room, she'd react strongly to changes in her routine, and she'd get angry instead of being frustrated when things didn't go according to plan. We watched everything and wrote down what seemed pertinent, waiting for her appointment to see Dr. Gaede. We hoped that the appointment would bring an answer or explanation for all the little changes we saw in Grace.

***

And now, here I was, on the other side of that appointment, and I was lost. I was afraid of the diagnosis Dr. Gaede had given me. Grace had changed, and yet not changed, for me in a matter of minutes: before the appointment, she was forgetful but delightful; now, I was inclined to think of her as a sick person. Sometimes it would be easy to forget, but then the significance of her diagnosis would hit me. When I sat with Grace, I felt consumed by the words *Alzheimer's disease*. I wanted to blurt them out to Grace and have her firmly explain that they had nothing to do with her. I wanted to see her get angry and challenge me, just so I could believe her and push the dreaded words away from me.

For the first time, I looked back on that fight over her car keys and took hope. During that fight, Grace had shown her tenacity, the same tenacity that had seen her travel alone through Europe, that had gotten her to the Great Wall of China at eighty-one. It was Grace's tenacity that would get us through this diagnosis together. And while I hadn't known it at that time, the fight for car keys had prepared me for life with Grace after she was diagnosed with Alzheimer's disease. The fight established the rules of engagement that would make being Grace's caregiver easier. We had faced off and survived without any casualties. It was the first time that she and I had found ourselves on opposite sides of a serious discussion, and it made me realize that being Grace's friend and daughter-in-law at the same time was not always going to be possible. At first, I resented this. It was hard for me to deny Grace anything, and I didn't like being cast as the enemy. But the more I puzzled over the divide between friendship and family, the more I could see that Grace had understood it all along. For Grace, *family* wasn't a noun; it was a verb, an action word. It was about relationships. She and I had become family long before Peter and I had gotten married. I'd felt it that first night we'd met, when she made it easy for me to talk about Peter. And since then, a hundred times, a thousand times, Grace had offered support and protection in equal measure. Our discussion over the car was the first time that Grace had ever fought me; she hadn't hidden anything; she hadn't put aside her feelings to be polite. She'd learned that I would be waiting to talk when she was ready. We had a stronger relationship because of that fight. Negotiating our way out of that conflict had been hard because we hadn't done it before, but now I understood Grace's anger better, however rarely I saw it, and knew how best to respond to her tensions. And Grace knew that she could be totally honest with me.

Pamela, Peter, and I agreed by consensus not to talk to Grace about the diagnosis. Peter and I could still remember how strongly Grace had responded to the words when she had caught Peter saying them, and Dr. Gaede suggested that, if the diagnosis aggravated Grace, there was little point in mentioning it to her. He had warned us all that there was little to be done for Grace's symptoms, and that the real work was in managing her needs. This advice laid the groundwork for the next stage of our lives together.

Chapter Four

The Struggle for Adaptability

Adaptability is a survival mechanism. We adapt to the circumstances of our lives, sometimes taking more, sometimes less. When resources become limited, we focus on surviving. When circumstances improve, we find time for pleasure; we move past survival and start to live again. It can be easy to adapt to negative circumstances because usually there is no other choice. When there is nothing to be had, it is easy not to take. Adaptability is what determines our success in life. Without it, we are trapped by circumstance.

Adaptability is a strategy for success, one that demands effort before it rewards us. We have to work to adapt ourselves effectively; we have to understand our environment and our goals before we can see the successful path forward. And there is never one path. The path forward is always changing as our world and goals change. So the work of adapting is never complete. It is the process of a lifetime.

Adapting to Grace's Alzheimer's disease has made me a contortionist. I've had to learn to see the world from her vantage point and to anticipate the needs she isn't able to articulate. I've had to learn to balance her needs with my own. For a long time, I thought that Grace's needs were my only priority. I demanded more for Grace and less for myself, and I felt sure that I had struck a good balance. But somewhere along the way, it stopped being an adaptation and started being a liability. At some point, we have to stop surviving and start living for ourselves again. We cannot survive on less for long. That is why our limit exists: to force us to make changes, to find better circumstances for ourselves. Adapting forces us to demand more for ourselves, and only in that way can we give more to others.

***

When Grace was first diagnosed, Dr. Gaede gave me one very simple instruction. He said, "You are the patient now. Take care of you and you will be doing the best thing possible for Grace." At that time, I didn't really hear him. I was looking for other kinds of instructions: "Get her on a schedule. Watch her take her medications. Make sure she stays active." I wanted to understand this game; I wanted to feel sure of myself. I read books about Alzheimer's disease, but when I compared their advice, I'd find the authors at war with each other. The first author would declare, "You are the authority. You must be consistent with your patient and enforce a regular schedule." Then the second would offer a rebuttal: "The patient needs flexibility—do not push them to do things they do not want to do. Accept their moods and let them set their own schedule." Confused, I'd consult a third writer, who would invariably say something like "Flexibility is essential, so long as a fixed schedule is closely adhered to!" Sometimes these conflicting instructions would reduce me to exasperation. The diagnosis was frightening and confusing, and for all the books and pamphlets I had collected, it seemed there was no absolute plan for me to follow. And it felt like it was up to me to somehow lead the family, especially Peter and Pamela, in caring for Grace.

Off the top of my head, I could recite Grace's health card number, her weight and height, her doctor's name. I could rattle off her vaccination record; I knew what surgeries she'd had and when. I went to Grace's doctor's appointments and I helped her make decisions about her medical care. There was never a discussion about who would step in as Grace needed more help; through a silent nomination process, I was chosen as Grace's primary caregiver. In truth, I nominated myself, and Peter and Pamela were glad for me to do so. I first involved myself in Grace's care when I asked her, after Peter and I moved to Calgary, if she wanted company going to the doctor, for an appointment I had arranged. After that, Grace's health was something I monitored. After Bob died, I could see that she was losing weight, and when I asked her about it, she confessed that she wasn't cooking for herself or eating as much anymore. It was easy for us to talk about these things, and I got used to being part of her life in that way.

My friendship with Grace prepared me to be her caregiver, and out of love for her, I never thought of refusing or pushing the responsibility onto someone else. It was a decision I made consciously, one that Peter and I discussed as best we could. Peter could see the time and energy that I spent helping Grace, and while he appreciated it, the guilt that he felt over it was harder to talk about. It was easy for me to help Grace because of the friendship between us, and so I did, always aware that my help sometimes relegated Peter to the sidelines. He was always available to me as a sounding board, offering suggestions and support, but it was increasingly clear that I was the first authority in Grace's life. Sometimes, rarely, he admitted that he felt guilty for not being the one to juggle Grace's needs and wants, and I had to reassure him that it was a choice I made for myself as well as for him and for Grace.

In the months after the diagnosis, when we were figuring out a care schedule for her or renewing her medications, Peter would shake his head and smile at me, marveling that I could pull her dates and details from the air. When I would outline a problem or a conflict, he'd listen, and after a pause, he'd turn to me and say, "Well, first things first: what do you think we should do?" Sometimes, I was ready for this question, ready to test my ability to guess what Grace might want or need from us. I'd take a deep breath before launching into the details of the plan I'd been tracing in my mind. I always felt nervous though, worried that I'd missed something or that someone would find an error in my planning. I would read out my list of things that needed attending, and we would talk about each task before deciding who would manage it. If it wasn't immediately clear, I'd put a circle beside it and leave it for later. And later, I'd write my own initials in and add it to my schedule for the week. It was easy to do this, for the most part. Because I was my own boss at work, it was easier for me to organize my schedule around Grace and catch up on work later in the day. It was less stressful than leaving a task unspoken for, expecting someone else to make the time to do it. I prided myself on managing all parts of Grace's care, and I kept the most important jobs for myself. It was my way of being sure that everything was done right.

I had managed my own company for six years, and I knew how to designate in my professional life, but when it came to Grace, I was afraid of making any error at all. I felt responsible for her life and her happiness, and I knew that responsibility would grow daily as the disease developed. And figuring out what she needed was difficult because I never discussed the disease with her; I was always guessing what she needed and kicking myself when I was wrong. I could predict what might set her off, and I had figured out what to do to calm her down. I wish my confidence in myself was growing, but during the first year, it wasn't. I found myself making mistakes and upsetting her without meaning to. Once I rushed her to finish her lunch, and she glared and snapped at me before turning back to me with a smile on her face as if nothing had gone wrong at all. Once I got stuck in a long line at the bank with her, and she started making loud and pointed comments about the tellers, refusing to stop as I tried to distract her. I tried to find humor in our family situation, but at times, smiles were few and far between as Grace became harder to read.

Every time I failed to predict what she would need, I got a little more worried that the others, who spent far less time with her, wouldn't be able to handle her. I felt nervous for them and for Grace; I knew how hard it was on Grace when she got agitated. I worried about what might happen when I wasn't there, and so I took as much of the responsibility as I could, insisting to myself that it was just easier for me to do whatever needed to be done. On the days when I had plans and new care ideas to share, I felt glad that the others looked to me for answers. I felt confident that I was doing a good job with Grace.

There were other days, though, when I would outline a problem and dread the moment when Peter would offer my own questions back to me. Days when all I had to offer was confusion. I was the in-house authority on Grace's disease, and I didn't know how to admit when I had no answers. In the months after the diagnosis, we were all still grappling with what Alzheimer's disease would mean for Grace. None of us knew what to expect from her as the disease developed or even what the next stage of the disease might look like. It was hard to tell the difference between a bad day and an evolving symptom. I didn't want to assume that every bad mood was really the disease peeking through, but I was afraid to dismiss anything out of her normal sweet character as unimportant. I worried privately. I kept my fears to myself, and I tried to be positive when the others raised concerns. When I had to admit that there was a problem with some aspect of Grace's care or behavior, some problem that I couldn't solve or explain, I felt like I had failed us, Grace most of all. I seemed confident to Peter and Pamela, but the routine shifted too often for me to ever feel really sure of myself. I didn't want to be the reason that we lost more of Grace than we needed to.

Most of what I learned from my research about Alzheimer's disease scared me, but early on, I clung to one very tantalizing idea: that it was possible to slow the progression of the disease. Some of the books glossed over this concept; others went into detail about how diet and exercise might help patients improve memory function. When I asked Dr. Gaede about this, he looked at me kindly and paused before answering. "That's not a simple question, Connie. It's different for every patient. You need to remember that for Grace, this isn't a new disease. It's been a part of her for years, developing a little bit at a time. It's impossible to notice the damage as it occurs. It's only once the damage to a specific part of the brain becomes widespread that the effect becomes evident. In a case like this, it's too late to start recovering Grace's memories. There's not enough foundation to start rebuilding." As soon as he was finished, my lips pressed together, my mind trying to formulate an argument that could counter what he said. I wanted to insist that something could be done, but he lifted one hand gently off the table and held it up in the space between us as if asking me to pause. He spoke again. "I understand that you want to fight me on this, Connie. I know that you want to think that you can fix this, but you need to know that this isn't something that can be fixed. This can't be changed. This disease is a reality for Grace, and you need to accept that." He paused, and we stared at each other for a moment as his words filtered through my determination. I felt my chin drop a little toward my throat. My breath snaked quietly out of my chest. "Now, Connie, I'm not trying to take away your hope. Keeping Grace active is important now, so is making sure her diet is balanced. There's plenty that you can do to help her and to slow down the next stages of the disease, but you can't expect that anything will change her diagnosis. It's not fair to put that pressure on yourself or on Grace." He leaned back and studied my face as I weighed his words. I tried to find an argument to defeat his logic, but nothing came to me. I nodded and sighed meekly before pushing the word "Okay" out of my throat. I could see his point about putting pressure on Grace, but there was so little I could do to help Grace now, it felt impossible to give up hope that something might make a small difference.

We all kept up hope that little changes might help Grace. Peter brought me instructions for exercises to help Grace keep mobile and independent. Pamela mailed puzzles and word searches to Grace after reading that they were a good way of stimulating brain cells. I think we all wanted to find a way to make a difference to Grace, to guarantee her a better future than the diagnosis had promised. I explained to Peter that Dr. Gaede had warned there was no hope of improvement but that we could try to slow the disease's development by improving her overall health. I repeated this speech to Pamela on the phone days later, emphasizing maintenance rather than improvement. When I went to Grace's house to help her cook meals for the week, I felt a bubbling satisfaction knowing that she was eating "super foods" off the list I'd found online. We started doing the recommended exercises together, and as her endurance increased, I couldn't help but look for signs that her mind was getting stronger as well. For several weeks, I saw improvement everywhere, tiny but significant to me. She breezed through a trip to the grocery store, unconcerned by the long lines. As we listened to the radio together, she named the song faster than I could. For a week, she didn't call me at work, consumed with worry about her purse. Because I wanted so much to see massive improvements, I read it into these little details.

After dinner together one night, Peter walked Grace home and returned to help me clean up the kitchen. I asked him if he noticed anything different in Grace. His answer was low, careful, but quick. "No . . . . Did you notice something? She seemed fine to me, but you spend more time with her, did you see a problem?" He watched me expectantly.

I bristled at his answer a little. "Problem? I'm not talking about a problem. I thought she seemed good. Better, even. Didn't she seem better to you?" My voice went tight, higher than usual. I pulled the cloth off the drying hook, held it under the tap for a moment, and started wiping down the counter, all while avoiding Peter's gaze.

When he spoke, I could hear his confusion. "Better? How could she be better? I thought—"

I cut him off, flinging down the cloth and shaking my head. "Never mind. Forget it. Forget I said anything." I stalked off, feeling angry that Peter had challenged me, that he hadn't seen improvement.

The next day, I got a panicked call from Grace insisting that she had left her purse at our house, that she couldn't find it anywhere, and I felt the same anger bubble up, although I held it back more carefully for Grace than I had with Peter. I suggested that she look for it in the places she usually found it—most often hidden in a cupboard or closet. When she found it and insisted that someone else must have put it away for her, I hung up and felt the careful enthusiasm of weeks dissolve into nothing. And I cried at my desk over the bitter disappointment of finding that Dr. Gaede was right. That phone call from Grace was routine now, and it epitomized my feelings about this disease. Alzheimer's disease sometimes left Grace confused and frustrated. I could never stay ahead of Grace's stress; I could never be prepared enough to prevent minor traumas. All I could do was field her calls and be ready for her panic to suddenly become mine, always with the belief that every second I took to resolve her problem, I was failing her. Some days, with my desk piled with unfinished work and deadlines looming, the sound of the phone ringing at all made me tense. Grace's calls felt, some days, like the bell at the beginning of a prize fight. It was a grudge match between me and the disease, both of us grappling wildly for control of Grace. And at the same time, I was always fighting for control of myself as well. The harder I had to fight to calm Grace, the harder I had to work to stop myself from panicking at seeing Grace move a little further down the path, a little closer to the disease. It was exhausting.

When I look back, I can see that life was easier once I stopped expecting Grace to be the exception. The Alzheimer's rule book was hard enough to understand without me hoping that I could find some provision to let Grace escape the disease altogether. I didn't know how to accept that there was nothing to be done to help Grace now that she had the disease. The diagnosis made me falter and made me question myself. The day Grace was diagnosed, one of the anchors in my life suddenly dropped away and everything began shifting. I wanted a care plan that could give me back a sense of balance. I wanted to feel that I was capable of handling Grace's needs and wants, but no matter how hard I tried, I couldn't control her disease. And so I began to adapt to living with questions and fears that could never be properly put away.

Because the disease scared me so much, at times it was hard to see past it and remember that, for Grace, nothing had changed. Because she and I were so close, she was generally glad for my company, but she was still an independent woman, and since Bob's death, she had gotten used to being responsible for herself. It was a point of quiet pride with her, and sometimes, especially when we were together at her house, she would gently chastise me for doing things for her that she could do for herself. Sometimes, despite myself, I would think of Grace as sick, and my instinct was to step in and take care of her. It took a long time for me to get used to the double vision that being Grace's friend and caregiver required. I had to learn to put aside my worries about the future when we were together and see all the ways that Grace was still able to be independent. I had to learn to give help when it was needed while also giving Grace the opportunity to manage things for herself. One of the first significant battles I faced began when Grace started planning for her return to Palm Desert, where she and Bob had spent their winters after Bob's retirement. The house they bought in Palm Desert was part of a small community of retirees who were generally content to amble their days away together in the central courtyard or on the neighboring golf course. The house itself was bright and airy and faced out onto a small duck pond framed by palm trees. Beyond the pond was the ninth green of the golf course and the clubhouse, where neighbors met for meals and social events. Grace loved being in Palm Desert; when she was there with Bob, they split their days between golf and gardening and the clubhouse, and Grace would call Peter and me in Calgary each week to update us on the lives of all her neighbors. The first winter after Bob died, Peter and I wondered how Grace would feel going down there without him, but when we asked about it, she smiled and assured us that she would be fine on her own. "I can feel the snow on the way," she exclaimed, wagging a finger at us. "That's my cue to head south. All the neighbors will be waiting for me, and who will take care of my garden if I'm not there?" And so she went, and we soon realized that she was fine in Palm Desert on her own.

However, once we got the diagnosis of Alzheimer's disease, it was hard for me to feel good about Grace being in Palm Desert without someone with her. I talked to Dr. Gaede about Grace's winter routine, and he said that it was fine for her to spend time there alone, so long as we checked in on her regularly and kept in contact. In his office, I had accepted it, rationalizing that Pamela lived relatively close by and we knew many of Grace's friends down there as well, but watching Grace packing for her trip, I felt conflicted. And beneath the conflict, I felt afraid. In my mind, Grace was at risk; she lived on her own in Calgary, but we were just minutes away, close enough to be able to help her with anything she needed. When she was in Palm Desert, we were hours, if not a full day, away from her, and the diagnosis of Alzheimer's disease made that distance seem even greater. I felt responsible for her health and happiness, and I was afraid that I might miss something if she were far away, out of my reach.

The real problem was that the more I held back my concerns, the more extravagantly I worried. Despite the doctor's assurances, despite knowing that there were other people I could rely on in Palm Desert, it still felt like letting Grace go was a significant risk, and I wasn't yet confident enough in myself, or in Grace, to handle it easily. Grace sensed my worry and teased me, saying that I needed more time on my own to relax and enjoy myself. In those moments, I would hug her and feel the strange intersection of my emotions: encompassing love for her, nostalgia for the simpler days of our relationship, and fear of the future I could not talk to her about. Of course, in the end, there was no way to stop her and no real reason to do so other than my own worries. And so I flew down to Palm Desert with her and got her settled in for the season: buying groceries, pulling weeds, and sharing lemonade. Grace and I had done this trip before, and the routine felt so familiar that my worries started to fade. I could see that Grace was happy here, surrounded by people who were glad to help with anything she needed. Palm Desert was home for her not just because of her friends but because it reminded her of Dividend, where she grew up, and of Bob, because this was where they spent the most time together. Something about this place amplified her already cheery disposition. Seeing Grace sitting in the garden, smiling and chatting with her neighbors while shielding her eyes from the sun, I realized that my fears about the future had distracted me from seeing what she needed from me today. For now, I needed to support Grace in taking care of herself and let go of the idea that she needed my full-time attention. She was safe here and happy, and that was all that mattered to me. And so I arranged a regular schedule of visits from family and friends, hugged Grace tightly, and flew home, promising to return in a few weeks. The next day, when I called Grace to check in, the energy in her voice assured me that I had done the right thing in letting go just a little. There were still moments when I worried about the distance between us; Grace would still call me every so often, anxious and in need of reassurance, but I learned to rely on my network of friends and family in Palm Desert to ensure that Grace was well supported. And of course, I visited her regularly, flying down to spend the weekend with her and see for myself that she was okay. It was the best compromise that I could manage; I would have many years to be Grace's caregiver, and knowing that, I tried to relish the moments when I could be her friend first.

One of the strangest things about life after the diagnosis was not being able to talk to Grace about what was happening. The more I learned about Alzheimer's disease, the more I wished I could confer with Grace about her symptoms, but it was impossible to ask direct questions without making her defensive about her memory, so I said nothing to her. Because I was muzzled, the topic of Alzheimer's disease was often on my mind. Some days, I would watch her carefully and see no symptoms at all; other days, expecting nothing, she would surprise me by repeating the same question over and over again. I could never predict these moments of confusion, and when they happened around others, they made me intensely uncomfortable. As Grace's primary caregiver, I felt responsible for smoothing over the awkward moments of the disease. I was afraid that, if I didn't explain her behavior, someone might make a comment that would make her self-conscious. When we were with other people, even with family, I felt stressed when Grace repeated herself as if her momentary lapses would be used against her. In an effort to protect her, I would hover around her conversations and jump in when she seemed to be struggling or when her answers stopped making sense. Because I couldn't talk to Grace, I learned to talk about Grace, in hand gestures and whispers, trying to explain away a disease that I still couldn't really understand. It was exhausting, but it felt necessary. I wanted to protect her from feeling foolish and exposed and protect myself from the realization that the disease was becoming more significant. There were still so many questions I couldn't answer and situations I didn't know how to handle. When Peter and I talked about it, we agreed that we couldn't protect her from everything and that there would be moments of chaos, but it was hard for me to let those moments play out without intervening. I didn't want to see Grace's confusion echoed in the faces of our family and friends as they watched her memory fail. I was afraid that at that moment, everyone would turn to me for explanations and encouragement, and I would have nothing to give them. I managed her conversations because I was afraid that, if I didn't, my own confidence would unravel and we would all become lost.

Of course, I shouldn't have worried. Grace's memory loss never caused a catastrophe. Things were never as precarious as they seemed. And once I could see that, I understood that I didn't need to work so hard to cover over the disease. That realization arrived one night over dinner with Don and Cynthia. Peter and I invited Grace as well because she loved formal dinners and knew Don and Cynthia well. As we were settling around the table with our plates and wine glasses, Grace began singing quietly under her breath, a song that I didn't recognize. I glanced around the table with an indulgent smile, knowing that I didn't need to excuse the song but wanting to make sure that everyone would be patient as Grace sang. Once she stopped singing, she looked up and me and smiled, and I felt a flush of love for her. "That was lovely, Grace, thank you," I said, picking up my glass to toast our guests. Grace beamed at the table as we clinked glasses, and everybody began eating and chatting in earnest. A few minutes later, Grace began to sing again, louder this time, and we all exchanged amused smiles; everyone knew about Grace's Alzheimer's disease, and we were all happy to indulge her. When she got to the end, Peter asked her about the song, and she told him that it was a Mormon song she had learned as a girl. The table nodded at her explanation and again we returned to our meal. As I stood up to get seconds for Don, I heard Grace take a deep breath and begin to sing again, louder than before. I tried to distract her by asking if she wanted anything else, but she ignored me, her eyes fixed at a spot on the wall across from her seat. In that moment, it felt like everyone was looking to me, unsure of how to respond, and I felt myself tense as I tried to explain Grace's behavior quietly without saying anything that would upset Grace. "Sometimes she gets stuck on a topic. I'm sure she's almost done," I said, wishing that she would stop. I hated trying to talk about her as if she couldn't hear me, although she was fully immersed in her song at this point, still looking past us into the room beyond. Everyone nodded as I turned toward the kitchen with Don's plate in hand, but I still felt responsible and frustrated that Grace had chosen this moment to fixate. I heard the final lines of the song and closed my eyes, hoping that she had gotten it out of her system, but she began again. "Grace?" I asked, sure that, if I distracted her, she would forget about the song. "Grace, will you help me in the kitchen?" She broke off her song as she looked over at me and seemed to consider my offer, but then she shook her head and leaned back in her chair.

For a moment, it seemed that everything would settle back to normal, and when I heard Peter ask Cynthia about her work, I breathed deeply, feeling relieved. I came back to the table, happy to give my attention to Cynthia, who was in full swing telling a story about a work colleague. Grace seemed to be listening as well, which reassured me. However, as soon as Cynthia stopped talking, Grace began to sing again, in full voice. "Grace, please, now is not the time for singing, okay?" I said, intending to make a statement but instead lifting my voice at the end, making it a question. But her determination to sing was obvious, and I started to doubt that I would be able to make her stop. Peter and I exchanged helpless glances and turned, slightly embarrassed, to our guests, but they waved away our wordless apologies. Instead of trying to resume our conversation, Cynthia caught Grace's eye and started humming the melody that Grace was singing. Realizing that she now had a partner as well as an audience, Grace waved her hands at the rest of us to encourage us to join in. Don stood up from the table and retrieved his iPad from the pile of coats and bags at the front door; back at the table, he Googled the first line of the chorus and, surprisingly, was able to find the words to the old children's hymn, which he shared with us all. With Grace as the bandleader, her face flushed and excited, we sang the song together, and when we came to the final line, Grace cheered for us all and clapped her hands at our performance. Toasting her, we all lifted our glasses and laughed at our impromptu sing-along, and for a moment, I marveled that the world hadn't fallen apart. Grace complimented us and then settled back in her chair, looking satisfied. We finished our dinner and were halfway through desert when Grace began singing again, and this time, we all joined in with her and sang with gusto before laughing with pleasure at ourselves. We sang three or four more times before the night was over, taking our cue from Grace, who could not seem to let go of the song. Throughout, I marveled at how firmly the song was stuck in her mind, and later, in bed, I reflected on how much fun it had been to sing all together like that, something I hadn't done in years. It was a significant moment for me as a caregiver to realize that, instead of trying and failing to control Grace's actions, I could simply accept her impulses and join her in her fun. Instead of fighting to keep her quiet, I could sing along with her and enjoy a moment of silliness. It was a lesson that stayed with me, and that has helped me in countless situations since then. That evening, Grace taught me that I didn't need to manage every aspect of this disease or explain away her actions. Sometimes, the best thing to do is to share in her fun.

Learning to step out of the role of caregiver was difficult for me; I was afraid that, if I didn't monitor things closely, I might miss something important. Often, Grace's Alzheimer's disease created chaos, and so that's what I prepared for. But sometimes the chaos was harmless, and when I relayed the details to Peter over dinner, we would laugh over the antics that Grace would get up to in her "Alzheimer's moments." Alzheimer's disease made Grace forgetful and anxious, but it also made her bold, a quality that I loved in her. Sometimes, it was the moments when I could see the disease most clearly that I could also see Grace the most clearly. Grace, uninhibited and determined, could be a very funny woman, and there were times when I felt amused instead of panicked by her unexpected whims. Amidst all the difficult moments, there were times when all I could do was smile at Grace's daring. There are some stories about Grace and her Alzheimer's disease that perfectly encapsulate the woman she has always been, and my favorite of these is known in the family as "the shoplifting story."

It started as a mundane sort of day, full of errands and minor tasks, the last of which was a trip to the grocery store to get what we needed for dinner together that night. Grace's energy was flagging a little, but when I offered to run into the store on my own, she shook her head, so we walked in together, her hand tucked neatly over my arm. Our grocery store routine was well established: I pushed the cart while she held the list and read out the things we needed, and together, we ambled along nicely. Knowing Grace was tired, I tried to make sure that we didn't forget anything and have to circle back to any section, but halfway down the cereal aisle, the word *onions* flashed in my mind, and I paused, trying to remember whether I had any left at home. Grace, noticing my hesitation, waited patiently, her eyes sliding across the jars of jam that were arranged neatly on the shelf in front of her. As I stood there, trying to picture my kitchen cupboards, I watched Grace examining the jars and saw her reach forward to pluck a small gold and green tin from the shelf. She examined it for a moment before holding it out toward me so that I could see it. "Mint jelly!" she pronounced, smiling, and I nodded, distracted by my inability to conjure a recent vision of onions in my kitchen. She held the tin close to her again, admiring the fancy gold lettering.

"Mint jelly . . . that's for lamb, Grace," I replied. "We're having steak for dinner, but we could make a sauce if you'd like," I offered, and she considered it for a moment before sliding the tin of jelly back onto the metal shelf, turning it carefully so that the label faced outward in line with all the rest of the tins. Then she shrugged and looked back down over our list.

Seeing her distracted, I maneuvered the cart to one side and asked Grace to wait for me while I ran back to the vegetable section. She straightened her shoulders and nodded. "Of course. I'll wait right here for you," she said, and waved me off.

When I returned with a small bag of onions, Grace had pushed the cart down to the end of the aisle, and I could see her peering along the row of cashiers, looking at the lines of shoppers at the checkout. Halfway down the aisle, I called her name, and she turned and waved at me, then gestured to the box of cereal she had added to the cart. "It wasn't on the list, but . . ." she explained, and I smiled at her as I shifted the box in the cart to make room for the onions. Under the cereal, I saw a small tin with gold lettering and green tint: mint jelly. Looking up, I saw Grace watching for my reaction, but when I reached for the tin, she turned all her attention to her shopping list. "Do you need this, Grace?" I asked, holding the tin out toward her.

"Oh, I just liked the package. I wanted to show it to you. Isn't it pretty?" she asked.

"The colors are lovely," I responded, pausing to admire the lettering before putting them on the shelf at the end of the aisle, "but we almost never have lamb, so we can leave it for now."

Grace took a quick look at the shiny gold label before turning her attention back to the list; after a moment, she announced that all we needed now was bread. I pushed the cart around the corner toward the bakery, and after a moment, Grace followed me, zipping up her purse after putting the list away.

By the time we got home, Grace was quiet. Thinking that she must be tired, I settled her in a chair at the kitchen counter while I unpacked the groceries. Usually, Grace liked to help with dinner, especially when we were cooking for Peter, but this afternoon, she was content to sit and watch me. When I suggested that we set the table, she eased herself up from her seat to help me lay out the cutlery and napkins. Once that was done, I returned to the kitchen, leaving her to finish the table on her own. Grace loved fancy dinners, so whenever we ate together, we used linen napkins and lit candles—"elegant touches," Grace would call them. "I have the perfect thing for our centerpiece, Connie," she called from the hallway. "I just need some little candles."

"In the living room," I called back, and a minute later, I heard her pulling open the chest of drawers that held the candles.

A few minutes later, she presented herself in front of me, smiling proudly. "Let me show you the table," she said and offered me her hand for the short walk. When we rounded the corner, I could see the table, cutlery, and wine glasses laid out neatly, with a circle of tea light candles in the middle. And inside that circle was a gold and green tin, glinting in the gentle light. Mint jelly. The same tin that I had returned to the shelf a few hours before. And most definitely stolen. She must have tucked it into her purse while I wasn't looking, determined to have it. Before I could react at all, Grace clapped her hands together and laughed with excitement. "Doesn't it look lovely? It's just right for our table, don't you think? Peter will love it!"

And looking into Grace's bright face, I agreed. "It's beautiful, Grace. Just perfect."

Peter and I often laughed about that tin of mint jelly, although never in front of Grace. There was something about the design of the label that she just loved, and we left it as the centerpiece on our table for a long time after that night. Part of me was mortified that Grace had stolen something, even something as small as this; it was very unlike her, and I worried that it was a sign of some new set of symptoms. But it didn't happen again. And once I stopped worrying, I started to see it as a sign of her determination, and it made me glad to know that she would still chase after the things that she wanted. When we retold the story to family, we embellished the theft, imagining Grace looking surreptitiously left and right before slipping the tin into her purse like a practiced pickpocket. In reality, she probably didn't even think about it; she just saw it and liked it. And in the retelling, I am always the warden, taking the tin away from her once, twice, sometimes a third time for good measure. I've come to love the story and the laughter that surrounds each new telling. With so many difficult, confusing moments to face with this disease, it is a story that reminds me that there can be good moments too if we are willing to laugh and accept reality as it is. If we are willing to let Grace have her moments.

For the most part, my biggest challenge was learning to relax when I saw evidence of Grace's illness. My instinct was to try to maintain normalcy by covering over Grace's confusion or preoccupations, thinking that I was saving her from embarrassment. It was hard for me to realize that in those moments, I was also trying to protect myself from proof that Grace was slipping away from me. The more normal things seemed in her everyday life, the more easily I could convince myself that I could handle what lay in front of us. In some ways, Grace's good nature softened the sharp edges of her Alzheimer's disease and made it easier for me to handle her early lapses in memory and occasional lack of judgment. Even her worst moments of confusion felt manageable; she rarely cascaded into anger the way that many of the books described. As much as I struggled to know how to help Grace, I also came to rely on her good nature to filter her words and actions. And in time, I learned that Alzheimer's disease will eventually erode those filters in ways that can't be covered over or ignored.

I will always remember the first time that I felt myself at the mercy of Grace and her Alzheimer's disease, afraid of what she might say or do and aware that I could do nothing to stop her. It was a moment of pure panic, and in that moment, I extrapolated forward, imagining a future filled with similar conflicts with this new version of Grace. It began at the border crossing between Montana and Alberta. Grace and I were driving from California to Calgary in the van that Grace kept down in Palm Desert but could no longer drive. Rather than sell it, she offered it to her son, Rob, and when he accepted, it fell to me to bring it across the border. After three days of driving, Grace's enthusiasm for the trip was flagging. As we pulled into the line up for border inspection, I rolled my shoulders and sympathized with Grace as she rubbed her knee, which was swelling slightly from being bent for so many hours on the road. "Only a few hours to go Grace, and then we'll be home. We'll be through this in a flash," I said, trying to sound upbeat. Grace smiled wanly and nodded before turning back to look out of the window across the yellow hills that surrounded the crossing. Seeing her fatigue, I felt a rush of determination to get her home, but the line in front of us was barely moving. To distract myself, I turned my attention to our passports and the van registration, which was in Grace's name. It hadn't occurred to me that I would need any other documents to bring the van across the border, but as we sat waiting, I started to worry that I had overlooked something. I didn't say anything to Grace, but I leaned forward and pulled the insurance papers out of the dashboard, thinking that they might contain whatever information I would need to show the customs officer. After scanning everything quickly, I organized all the papers on my lap and resolved not to worry.

Twenty-five minutes later, I found myself being waved toward the window, hopeful that there wouldn't be a problem. But there was. After passing over our passports, I explained that Grace had bought the van in California years ago but now wanted to bring it into Canada for her son. The border officer listened impassively and shook his head, holding out the US export forms that I needed in order to bring the van through customs. "These should have been filled out in Great Falls, ma'am. I can't let the van through without the necessary paperwork," he explained, looking disinterested. When I asked what my options were, he sighed and shifted his weight in his seat. "You're going to need to go back to Great Falls and submit the paperwork for exporting this vehicle. They'll give you a document like this," he said, pointing at a form taped to the wall beside him, "and then we can process you. But until I have that document, there's nothing I can do for you." And with that, he sat back in his chair and seemed to excuse himself from our conversation.

I paused for a moment, trying to focus my thoughts. A quick glance at Grace assured me that there was no way we could turn around; she was rubbing her knee again, her face flushed in discomfort. Feeling my frustration—at Rob, at the border officer, even at Grace—rising, I turned back to the window. "Isn't there some way to expedite the paperwork or get a temporary permit for the van? There must be some way to allow us through. It's not reasonable to ask that we drive all the way back across the country," I said, trying to keep my voice even. Grace was very quick to pick up on my moods, and I didn't want to add to her stress by letting on that there was a problem.

The officer shook his head to emphasize that there was nothing he could do, but I waited, keeping my eyes on his, and after a moment, he picked up the phone and seemed to be explaining my situation to whoever was on the other end. When he finished, he gestured to the empty row of parking spaces in front of the border crossing building and said, "Park there. You can go over to the American agents on the other side and ask them if they can help you fill out the paperwork and give you what you need. If they can, then you can come back here." And he leaned back again and waved me toward the parking spaces.

As I rolled up my window and parked the van, I tried to make light of the situation for Grace, promising her that this would be a quick delay. But I was wrong. After two hours of explaining the problem to the American officers and waiting as they searched for possible solutions, there were no solutions. One officer suggested that I leave the van and arrange to fly home to Calgary with Grace; another said that I couldn't leave the van and would have to drive it back to Great Falls to get the papers sorted out. A third officer was sympathetic but agreed with the others that there was nothing they could do. Between suggestions, Grace and I sat together in the warm office, waiting for a solution to present itself. Grace kept asking when we could go back to the car, although I wasn't sure if she was repeating herself out of frustration or confusion. Either way, I felt responsible. I should have double-checked the rules for exporting vehicles across the border. I should have made sure I understood the requirements before we started driving. I tried to keep my voice even as I assured her that everything was fine, that we could go back to the car soon, but inwardly, I was starting to panic.

One of the American officers called me to the counter, and though I tried to convince Grace to stay seated, she followed me. She knew something was wrong, and her instinct was to stay right by my side, which increased the pressure I felt to find a solution for her. Standing at the counter with Grace, watching other cars being waved through into Alberta, I felt a burst of claustrophobia, wishing that Grace would sit down so that I could speak freely. Trying to stay calm in front her was exhausting. The officer explained that there was nothing she could do to help me with the paperwork, but seeing the strained look on my face, she leaned toward me and offered some advice: "Go back to the Canadian side and explain that you and your mother-in-law can't go back to Great Falls. They might be able to make an exception if you press them." She nodded toward Grace, who was standing uncomfortably beside me, and slid the empty forms back across the counter. I thanked her and tried to contain my disappointment as I led Grace outside.

I paused in front of the Canadian border office, trying to collect myself, and I heard Grace sigh deeply as I reached for the door. Closing my eyes for a moment, I summoned the last of my enthusiasm. "We're almost finished Grace. It can't be much longer." She didn't respond.

There were two officers inside the Canadian office, and after a moment, one gestured for me to come forward. Again, I tried to convince Grace to sit and wait for me, but she refused, so we approached the counter together. I explained that I didn't have the export papers for the van, that Grace and I had been driving for three days, that Grace needed to rest and couldn't turn around now. The officer listened, nodding, and as I heard myself explain the situation, I felt sure that something could be done. Driving back to Great Falls to collect a few signatures seemed ridiculous. Beside me, Grace shifted constantly, trying to relieve the pressure on her knees. When I finished speaking, the officer paused and then shook his head. "I can't let you through without the export papers for the van. The paperwork needs to be complete—no exceptions."

I felt a rush of anger and the pinch of possible tears, but knowing that Grace was already stressed, I held back. "Please, there has to be some way to make an exception. We've been driving for three days and my mother-in-law is exhausted. I need to get her home," I said. Without pausing to consider what I'd said, he repeated bluntly, "No exceptions."

I dropped my hands on the counter without saying anything, trying to keep my composure as I groped around for some idea of how to get Grace home today. After a moment, Grace cleared her throat, and I closed my eyes, waiting for her to ask me if we were going home now. Instead, she pointed a finger toward the customs officer and said loudly, "You are an asshole!" Silence descended around us for a brief moment as the officer and I both turned toward Grace, stunned.

"Excuse me?" he said accusingly, glaring at both of us.

I reached for Grace's hand, trying to pull her back from the counter, but she was rooted to the spot and wouldn't be moved. "You heard me. You're an asshole! You could be nice but you're not. You're being an asshole!"

The room seemed to shrink around me as I suddenly imagined Grace and I being rushed off to jail for attacking a customs officer. The officer pushed back his chair and stood up while Grace kept jabbing her finger toward him, saying, "Asshole! Asshole!"

"I've had enough of this, both of you!" the officer almost shouted.

I inserted myself between Grace and the officer. "I tried to explain to you, she has Alzheimer's disease and she's exhausted. I have to get her home. You can see the state she is in," I said, sure that he would see that it was all true. But he was too angry to listen to me; instead, he glared at Grace, who glared right back at him.

Thankfully, another officer stepped into the room, drawn by the commotion. She took in the situation as she hurried over to us. Her arrival distracted Grace, who stopped shouting, and the officer, who stepped back with his arms folded across his chest. She touched the first officer gently on the arm and said, "I've got this," and then she turned her attention to Grace. "Are you feeling all right, ma'am?" she asked, and after a pause, Grace looked up at her, smiled, and responded, "Yes, thank you."

The officer directed Grace over to the row of chairs and I sat down beside her, trying to breathe as my sense of panic slowly subsided. Grace turned her eyes on me and shook her head. "He was being very difficult, Connie. Why was he being so rude to you?"

"It's okay, Grace," I said, holding her hand gently, exhausted and struggling to contain my welling emotions. Grace hadn't ever gotten so angry with a stranger before, and it unnerved me to know that I hadn't seen it coming. I had been so busy trying to keep my own frustration in check that I hadn't realized how much strain Grace was under.

When I spoke to the new officer, my first words were strangled. "I'm sorry for this, it's just that Mom is so tired. I need to get her home. We can't turn around."

The officer nodded, and the look of understanding and sympathy on her face almost melted me. "I know it can be hard," she said, nodding at Grace before looking back at me and lowering her voice. "My mother has Alzheimer's disease too." The expression on her face told me that she understood what had happened, that Grace was angry and confused and too tired to mean any real harm. The relief of knowing that she understood my situation was palpable and I had to gulp back my breath to stop from crying on the spot. She sat down beside me and Grace and listened as I explained the situation. After a minute, she stood up and set me to work filling out a number of papers and offered Grace a drink of water. Ten minutes later, we were walking out the door with temporary permission to drive the van into Canada.

As we got into the van, I felt exhaustion hit. After all that had transpired, I still had to face the drive home, but at least we were going home to Calgary and not back to Great Falls. I turned on the air conditioning and the CD player for Grace, and sat, still sandbagged by the image of Grace glaring up at the customs officer, shouting "Asshole!" without a clue that she was putting us both in a dangerous situation. It was the first time that I'd lost control of Grace in public, and it was unsettling to know that I had missed the warning signs that she was running out of patience. It felt like the disease had snuck up on me while I was distracted, and now my confidence was significantly shaken. Too upset to think about it, I turned on the van and pulled out of the parking lot and back onto the highway. I tried to ignore the worry in the pit of my stomach, reminding myself that Grace was safe, which was all I could ask for.

I took a deep breath and smiled over at Grace, who smiled brightly back at me in return. Her next comment made me want to laugh and cry at the same time. Completely oblivious to everything that had just happened, she began to chat with me. "So, how was your day?" she asked, genuine curiosity in her voice. I looked at her and it dawned on me that, as quickly as her anger had arrived, her memory of being angry was gone. This shocked me a little and made me feel alone with my thoughts and concerns. As I turned my head away from Grace, the tears I had been holding back slid down my face. I knew that we were both safe now, but I could imagine what might have happened if the other officer hadn't stepped in and distracted Grace. The first officer didn't understand Alzheimer's disease; he didn't understand that Grace had been shouting because she was tired and confused. All he saw was a disruption, an angry old woman looking for a fight. How could I protect Grace when I couldn't understand her myself? Once again, my confidence in managing this disease had been shattered. Later, this would become another funny story, causing laughter and incredulity every time it was told because it was so entirely unlike Grace. At that moment, however, as long empty sections of prairie rolled by, I felt the weight of the border crossing dragging my spirits low.

Learning to live with Alzheimer's disease has always been like this: moments of confidence and success followed by moments of fear and failure. There are times that I know exactly how to help Grace and other moments when I am surprised by her wants and needs. My challenge is accepting that I will always be a little unprepared. Grace's life is logical to a point, but she has moments where no logic applies and all I can do is guess at how to help her. Often, I guess wrong, and then I have to accept that I've done my best and forgive myself for not always being right. Since the diagnosis, the ground beneath us is always shifting. I think Grace would understand my fears if I could explain them to her, and I often wish that I could talk to Grace about how much she scares me sometimes. But the blessing and the curse of this disease is that she rarely remembers her worst moments. She lives in the present, and to be with her, I have to do the same.

Chapter Five

The Need for Negotiation

Negotiation is about balance. It is about weighing needs and finding a compromise. Sometimes we negotiate with others, but most often, we negotiate with ourselves. We ask ourselves to walk farther, to carry more, with the promise that there will be a reward later. We strike deals with ourselves that we keep secret because we know that, if we shared them, others may point out that we are being unrealistic, that the burden we plan to carry is too great. We call it negotiation, but often there is no balance. There is only one-sided compromise.

Learning to negotiate with others requires that everyone's needs are considered. Some voices are easy to hear when they express need; others are more difficult. Some people are silent. By design or experience, some are deaf to their own needs; they say nothing about themselves when they sit down to negotiate. They don't notice that they have brought no demands to the table and so do not complain when they receive nothing. They leave the table burdened by unmet need. They leave the table unaware that they could ask for more. It is a skill to recognize need and respect it. The strategy of compromise depends on it.

In parts of my life, I am a good negotiator. I consider all sides and do what is fair. But when emotions are involved, when I am forced to negotiate with family, I falter. I don't like asking the people I love for help, so I don't ask. Instead, I negotiate with myself. I refuse to compromise with others, and so I compromise myself. For a long time, I lived this way. But the strain of Alzheimer's disease revealed the imbalance, the depths of what I refused to say, even to myself. Having to negotiate the needs of so many somehow taught me to recognize my own needs and to have the confidence to say them. Learning to carry the burden of Grace's disease taught me to share my burdens with others.

***

I think of myself as a strategist.

I remember the first time I realized this. I was young, still in middle school, and my mother, because of her religious beliefs, wouldn't let me join any of the afterschool sports teams. It wasn't a discussion; it was an edict. She would say nothing other than that she didn't approve of the spirit of competition. I brooded over not being allowed to play basketball or try out for track until it occurred to me that I might make more progress with my mother if I began to negotiate. I asked to join the chess club. I didn't know how to play at that time, but my older brother Bart played, and he always lorded his skill in chess over the rest of us. I once asked him why some pieces moved straight while others moved in specific patterns and why some pieces could move as far as they liked while some only got one or two jumps at a time. He rolled his eyes and explained that chess was too complicated for me to understand. He had no interest in sharing the game with me.

My mother resisted when I first raised the possibility of learning chess, but when I explained that I only wanted to learn, not play in chess competitions, she relented. With her permission, I stayed late after school the next day to ask Mr. Root, the chess team coach, if I could practice with the rest of the club. I shifted anxiously as he considered my request, and after a moment, he smiled and said that he could fit in one more student. I was thrilled with myself. It was the first time I had pushed for something just for me and it felt like a massive victory. From the first afternoon, as the coach explained the strengths and weaknesses of each piece on the board, I was captivated. I loved the simplicity of the board and the complexity of each move. The mechanics of the game made sense to me, and I didn't get lost in the mix of pieces spreading out along the chequered pattern of the board. I could see a path for each of my game pieces: I could see how my knight would dance past the soldiers of my opponent and then double back to catch them unaware; I could predict when to send my queen sailing across the board unimpeded to devastate my opponents' defenses.

The coach praised me for learning so quickly. After I won a game against a boy two grades ahead of me, he winked at me and said that I was a "natural strategist." I turned the words over in my mind on the walk home, feeling pleased to have earned this praise. At that time, I wasn't really sure what a strategy was—I took it to mean "plan." But when I played, it didn't feel like I had a plan. I just watched the board and I could see paths for each of my pieces. I could tell which moves would leave me open to attack and which would let me hide in plain sight, tucked safely beside my opponent's bishop or behind their pawn. It was exciting to discover that I had a talent—I didn't have any skill that set me apart, and I had never had anything to share when my friends bragged about how well they did at their dancing or music lessons. But I didn't brag about chess to anyone, even to my brother, who refused to play a game with me on the grounds that I couldn't possibly offer him any challenge. I told my mom that chess club was "okay" and left it at that. I liked having a secret skill, and I started to think of myself as a strategist, just like the coach had said. That word made me feel capable. It made me feel proud.

One afternoon, long after I had become familiar with the dim, afterschool classroom and the sound of felt-bottomed wooden pieces sliding across the chess boards, the coach asked me into the hall. He explained that one of the students had dropped out of the chess tournament that weekend and that he was one player short; if I got my parent's permission, I could fill in on the team and play in the competition. I still remember the feeling in my chest on the walk home, holding the permission form in front of me so that I could keep looking down to see my name written on the top of the page. I felt expansive. But my mother didn't understand my enthusiasm. When I burst into the house, pushed the form in front of her, and breathlessly related what the coach had said, her face didn't change. "We agreed that you could join the club, Connie, but that's it. I don't want you competing," she said. She wouldn't say anything but that. I began to bargain with her, promising that I would work harder in school and do more at home to help her. I tried to think of our conversation as a game of chess, and I looked hard for the weakness in her logic, but I couldn't see her rationale at all. In the end, I convinced her out of sheer determination. When I placed the slightly rumpled but signed permission form on Mr. Root's desk, he nodded and grinned at me, and I thought to myself that being a strategist might be a useful skill.

I remember very little of the tournament day—the nervous tension, the sense of awe when I saw the gymnasium packed full of people, and the chess tables lined up on a low stage under bright humming lights. But I remember the game itself. I remember Mr. Root explaining that the coaches matched up players of opposing teams according to skill, and I remember being given the number eight, which meant I was the weakest player on my team. I was glad of that number because it meant that I would play against another new player. Whatever happened, that number promised me an even matchup, which helped to keep my nerves under control.

However, just before we all sat down, Mr. Root came over to me and explained that he needed to switch my number. That he needed me to play someone else. I held my number tightly and nodded, trying to be amenable, a team player. "Okay," I said and held out my hand to trade the new number for the old. Mr. Root smiled at me kindly and pointed to the only table with an empty chair. Table number one. I didn't say anything even though I felt panic rushing through me. Why was this happening? Why was I playing at the first table? I looked across the room at table eight, where my would-be opponent was sitting in her seat, her short legs kicking the chair legs, her fingers twirling her hair nervously. Why couldn't I play her?

The whistle blew then, so I ran to the only seat left as the announcer began reviewing the rules: "Two points for a win, one point for a draw. The highest overall score for the team will decide the winning school." When I looked up, I realized that my opponent was looking confidently across at me. I remember him telling me that last year, he had won a medal for best individual player. I remember thinking that I was the only person on my team whose opponent was notably older. I remember looking at the board, unable to imagine my pieces moving. They seemed nailed to the spot. When the word "Begin!" boomed through the high ceilings of the gym, all the players leaned in to their games. I tapped the timer to begin and picked up a pawn. The first few moves went quickly as we opened up the board and began testing each other. Soon enough, our pieces had spread out across the chequered pattern, and the game started to distract me from my nerves.

I didn't take a full breath during the entire game, but my hand stopped shaking visibly each time I picked up a game piece. As my opponent considered each next move, I imagined my pieces testing different paths across the board and looked for the cracks in his defenses. I could hear other games ending around me, the quiet grunts of victory and the scrape of chairs as the players stood up. As my queen started stalking his queen around the board, I realized that most of the players from my school were finished and that a small crowd was gathering around my game, waiting and watching. A shiver ran through me as I became aware of the crowd, but staring hard at the game, I felt the crowd recede into the background again. I could see that the game was almost over, that I needed to corner him and take out his last strong pieces—his queen and his bishop—or my own defenses would be stretched too thin and I would lose my advantage.

I pushed forward with my rook, leaving my own last bishop open. I saw his eyes flash, thinking that I'd made a mistake, and he picked up his queen and hovered it over my bishop for a moment before knocking my piece over. The crowd around us was quiet except for a collective intake of breath when my piece tipped over. His eyes were on me, and I looked up at him and nodded gently. And then I smiled. I picked up my rook, so that its base was hovering just off the board. As I moved it across the board, I felt almost jittery as I tipped his queen over and let my rook rest on her square. There was a chortle from somewhere at the back of the crowd as someone realized my gambit. I felt proud because this was a good game. We were both playing well. For the first time, it occurred to me that I might win. I didn't care about winning for myself, but the idea of helping the school team to win suddenly left me breathless. When I sat down, I felt winning was impossible; now, it seemed almost likely.

I gritted my teeth and turned back to the game, feeling a hot wave of determination. I made a good move and another good move. Then at my next turn, I looked hard at the board and could see no clear move. There was nowhere to go that wouldn't weaken my position. It was something I hadn't faced before, and I didn't know what to do. Knowing I had to move something somewhere, I made a move. The boy across from me moved as well, and I started to realize that neither of us could defeat the other. After four moves, the coach on the other team signaled to my coach, and they studied the board for a minute before nodding, and leaning down to both of us. "Neither of you are able to put the other in checkmate, so this game is going to be called a draw, okay?" the other coach said, looking between us.

Mr. Root stood back and said loudly into the crowd, "The game between the first players is officially a draw."

The crowd clapped and cheered, and the coach for the other team said, "Well done to you both," patting his player on the back and smiling at me broadly. I tried to smile back, but I felt devastated. All I thought was that, by not winning, I had failed and disappointed my whole team.

I didn't dare look at them; I was sure that I'd be met with scorn. I sat in my chair as the crowd moved away, toward the top table of judges who were tallying each school's score. The buzz of excited chatter was everywhere, moving so quickly that it passed right over me. Ignoring it, I looked at the game board, trying to reverse each move to find my mistake. Where had I gone wrong? I stared hard at my rook as the image began to blur. A tear dropped onto my arm and my body flinched as I realized that I might cry in the middle of this gymnasium. My hands gripped my jeans and I sat up tall, afraid to let this defeat crush me in public. I breathed in through my nose and my hands reached forward, lining the dismissed pieces up into place on the board. I wanted to look busy, to be busy—too busy to notice that I had failed. I had almost all the pieces in place when the chair opposite me slid back. Mr. Root sat down, watching me evenly. I didn't know how to meet his eye as I screwed up the courage to apologize.

"I'm sorry that I lost," I said, and I blew out all my breath and sat as still as I could.

I waited for a response, and in the seconds that ticked by, it suddenly occurred to me that Mr. Root might be angry, not disappointed. The thought choked me. I heard him lift out of his chair, and I thought that he might be walking away, but then I saw his feet beside me. He knelt down so that he could see my face, and when I looked at him nervously, he was smiling, shaking his head. "Connie, you didn't lose. It was a draw—that's a very different thing in chess! That happens when two players are so evenly matched that they play each other into a corner, until there are no moves left. And you have to remember who you were playing. That boy has had much more practice than you. He's been coming here for at least three years! You got a point for our team, and you took that point from one of the best players here!" There was a pause, and then he continued. "Connie, you should be playing on the team. That means you'll have to start coming to all the competitions. Do you think you can do that?"

My head bolted upward. "On the team? Really? I'd love to be on the team!" My chest was a traffic jam of emotions.

Mr. Root laughed gently. "It's been a big day for you, Connie, and you've done really well. I'd say you're a natural at this game. The team needs someone like you!"

When he said that, every other noise in that giant room dropped away. I turned his last sentence over in my mind as I sat there, in awe of the idea that the team could "need" me. At home, I was the oldest girl, which meant I was the babysitter, the cook, the cleaner. What I wanted was to have a talent, and suddenly, I had one. It made me feel invincible to be called a natural. Mr. Root and I stood up then, and after he was sure that I was okay, we moved away from the chess tables toward the crowd at the front of the room, where the announcer was explaining the breakdown of points awarded to each school. In truth, I didn't care what the announcer said. I was brimming over with an enthusiasm that was new to me, that I hadn't felt before. I was special. Me. As the announcer got closer to the top of the list, the other players on the team slid through the crowd to be closer to the coach and squeezed my hand as they found a place to stand, whispering "Nice game" and "Isn't this exciting?" to me. I was in heaven. I had found a team; I was part of something.

The third and second place schools were announced and the players ran up to the front to receive the plaque. I felt excited, happy. I was so busy grinning to myself and thinking about how it would feel to be a full member of the team at practice the next week that I didn't hear our school name being called out over the speakers. While the rest of the team bolted up onto the stage, the coach had to tap me on the shoulder and point toward the podium before I realized that we had won the prize for best overall team. Walking up the steps, I was careful; my hands lifted automatically up in front of me a little in case I fell forward. When the crowd clapped for us, I looked out across the gym and marveled that I was standing there under the bright lights, on a stage. We had won by two points, which meant that my game had been part of our win. It was the first glorious moment in my life.

I played with that chess team for the next two years. We played after school, once all the other kids had filed out and everything had become quiet. We paired off and laid out our game pieces, and soon, the room was filled with the sound of pieces moving across the board. Sometimes, we watched each other's games and discussed different move options out loud. At first, I was hesitant to speak, but after a few weeks, I risked it and found people nodding as I explained what piece I thought should be moved. Chess club gave me a forum to speak with authority, and it didn't take long before I could speak my mind clearly. We entered competitions, big and small, and I loved the challenge of each one. I learned to think through my nerves, to see the board clearly no matter what was going on around me. By the time I left the team, as our family was moving again, I had a bronze, silver, and gold medal from the American Chess Federation. I arranged them neatly on a shelf in the bookcase in my room. I kept them on display even after I left the chess team because they reminded me that I did have a talent. I was a natural strategist.

***

We all seek strategies to help us navigate. My unexpected ability to navigate the chessboard left me with a residual sense that, no matter what life through at me, if I just studied the situation hard enough, I could find a strategy to deal with any challenge.

I thought about those medals early one morning while Peter was still asleep. I had my day planner open on my knees and I was flipping between pages, comparing my meeting schedule for the day with Grace's schedule for the week. Her calls to Peter and me were getting more frequent and frantic than in the past; some days, she called me five or six times and always started with "Connie? Connie? You know I hate to call you at work, but . . ." We had agreed that she couldn't be left alone every day, that one of us needed to visit her at lunch or schedule time to drop by in the afternoon, hence the schedule. There were circles drawn around each weekday and initials written in to indicate who was in charge of finding the time to visit her. Mine mostly, but also Peter's. Sometimes I could count on Colleen and Jean, Grace's sisters, to help out with the scheduling while they visited Grace. But today's circle was empty. I had interviews scheduled back-to-back at work as I was hiring a new operations manager. I had intended to find someone to spend some time with Grace, but it had slipped my mind until this morning, when I had woken up with the distinct feeling that I wasn't prepared for my day. As I looked at the calendar, however, I realized the problem wasn't with work but with Grace's schedule. I looked at Peter, who was sprawled on the bed, turned away from me, and dismissed the idea of waking him. It was only five thirty, and he wouldn't need to be up for another hour. And I knew he had meetings all day today anyway. I sighed and pressed my hands across my face, trying to feel awake. It was pointless to stay in bed, wasting time, so I dropped my feet onto the floor and stood up, picking up my datebook along the way.

In the living room, I settled onto the couch and pulled a woven blanket over my legs. Opening my schedule again, I turned to the empty circle and inwardly cringed. I tried to see an opening where I could slip away to see Grace. The office wasn't too far away if my timing was right. But I could see no opening. It was that thought that brought the chess medals to my mind. They'd been packed away for years now, but the image of them propped up on my shelf as a kid floated in front of me for a moment. Maybe I used to be better at strategy, I thought, feeling frustrated. I would have to choose between priorities—time with Grace or my responsibility at work. The thought made me angry, although not at anyone in particular. Increasingly, I had to make this kind of decision, and no matter what I chose, it felt like I chose wrong. Halfheartedly, I thought back to my early chess competitions, when I'd had the satisfaction of knowing my next move before my opponent had pulled their hand back from the board. I wished I could feel that sure again. And that's when it occurred to me that my problem was indeed a strategy problem. I was chasing two pieces at once instead of finding a way to corral both. What I needed was to be at work and be sure that Grace was occupied and safe. Couldn't I take her to work with me and find a job for her? Wouldn't that let me accomplish both objectives? My head tilted to the side as I thought about it, and I chewed on my lower lip. There were lots of things she could do and I could see her in between interviews; we could even have lunch together. And I could tick off that circle on Grace's schedule without needing to cancel any interviews. The day suddenly felt manageable.

I hopped up and walked quickly to the bedroom, where Peter was still sleeping. I went around to his side of the bed and leaned in.

"Peter?" I half-whispered the first time, but I was too excited with my own cleverness to be more patient than that. "Peter, are you waking up?" I asked.

He opened one eye and squinted at me, offering a vague yes that was half statement, half question. It was enough for me, so I rubbed his shoulder to keep his attention and launched into the problem. When I paused, he adjusted the blanket and interjected, "You have a solution? Be in two places at once?" His voice trailed off as I shook my head and made a face.

"I'll bring her to work with me!" I announced proudly. "That way, she has some time out of the house, and I can check on her whenever I want to, and we can have lunch together."

Peter considered for a moment and then nodded, a sleepy half smile on his face. "That sounds good, as long as you're sure you can find something for her to do," he said, yawning.

I waved the words away. "Yes, yes, that's the easy part. You know her—she's great with people, she'll love it. This is great—my day just got so much easier!"

Looking at the clock on Peter's side table, I considered when to call Grace to explain the plan. I knew she might get a little flustered at having this pushed on her, so I wanted to give her time to get ready. Rolling out of the bed for the second time that morning, I felt much lighter.

When Grace and I arrived at work, I took her to my office and asked her to stamp envelopes while I set myself up for the day of interviews. She worked slowly but diligently, and every so often, she smiled at me and said something kind, like "This is a very impressive office Connie" or "Oh, don't you look good today—very elegant!" *Elegant* was one of her favorite words, and she said it in a very specific way, drawing out the vowel sounds so that it became "ellie-gan-tay." It was something that she had picked up in Italy when she was shopping for Presenting Italy, a joking affectation that was now more natural to her than the English pronunciation. Each time she said it, I would nod and agree—"Very ellie-gan-tay"—mimicking her, and then we would both smile.

Just before my interviews began, I walked with Grace down to the call center and explained that she had two important jobs: to hand out candy to each staff member in the call center and then greet staff as they came into the break room. She sat in the staff room all afternoon, talking to whoever was in there, and whenever someone new came into the room, she would introduce herself and ask how their day was going. More often than not, Grace found herself holding court, introducing one staff member to another, and then announcing "Isn't this fun!" as people smiled at one another. It wasn't the perfect solution but, having Grace with me, let me get my work done without being worried about her at home alone.

At the end of the day, I stuck my head in the break room where Grace was talking with my assistant. When she saw me, Grace smiled and held out her small basket of candy. "Oh, Connie—have a piece of candy!" She shook the basket, and I laughed and walked over to her to pick out a piece. My assistant nodded and eased gently out of the room as I settled in to talk to Grace.

"How was your day, Grace?" I asked. Though she couldn't remember all that she had done, she said she had been very busy with an excitement in her voice. I was happy to hear her so animated, but I could see that she looked tired. Being social, though a good distraction, took a lot of effort, and bringing her to work was not a permanent solution. On the drive home, she was quiet, and when I parked in her parking lot, she sighed deeply before leaning forward to pick up her purse. I offered to help her start dinner, explaining that Peter was working late too, and she smiled and said I should come up. I stayed for dinner and did the dishes as Grace got ready for bed. She laughed at herself for going to sleep so early, but I shook my head and said that "working girls" couldn't be up early and go to bed late. She liked that expression. I thanked her for her good work as I left, and she smiled again, pleased with herself.

It was just past 8:00 p.m. when I got in the door, and it was a relief to drop my bag and coat and take a full breath. Having Grace at the office was a solution with its own problems—it wasn't good for her to be so tired. I thought back to my feeling of satisfaction this morning and tried to remember that the alternative was to leave Grace alone all day, which was worse for her than fatigue. I needed another way to keep Grace safe, and that was going to require a whole new strategy.

One of the things I hadn't expected when Grace was diagnosed was how pervasive my authority in her life would become. At first, I had anticipated being in charge of her medical decisions and I felt I could handle that responsibility. I followed the advice of her doctors and took the most reasonable course of action. But there were areas of Grace's life where I was reluctant to step in. Grace was my friend, my equal, and it was hard to feel that I had the right to make personal decisions for her. I didn't want to use my authority until I absolutely had to, and I wasn't yet sure that I would know when that moment had arrived. But I was starting to see that Grace was compromised by the disease, unable to safely care for herself on her own. The disease had progressed, the board had changed and I needed to reanalyze the pieces.

Caring for Grace gave me the same sense of accomplishment that I had at sixteen when I'd taken on a double course load. It was a challenge to handle the demands of her Alzheimer's disease, but so long as I could cover the shortages, I could maintain the fiction that Grace's disease wasn't getting worse. I thought that I could manage the symptoms and so manage the disease, and for a while, it worked. Up to a point. And then, staring at my overloaded datebook, it dawned on me that it wasn't working anymore. I hated the feeling that my ship was sinking. I had already thrown so much overboard to try to keep Grace and myself afloat, but it didn't seem to matter; the water was still pouring in. Admitting it felt like accepting failure. But I couldn't find any more time to give Grace—I had taken time from work, from Peter, from myself, and now I had to accept that I had no more time to give her. Grace needed someone to check in with her a few times a day, to make sure she was remembering to eat, to get her out of the house for a few hours so that she didn't spend her days alone in her kitchen.

I had researched assisted living early on, after the diagnosis, but she hadn't needed that kind of help then. She still didn't, but it seemed like the only way to move forward. I could see only two options for us: either I cut back at work to be with Grace or I find a place for her in an assisted living facility close by. I thought about those two options for a long time, trying to find a path forward that would allow all of us to be happy. For moments at a time, I would convince myself that, if I changed my work schedule, I might be able to maintain the course, but logic always defeated me: we were now working on a sliding scale, and Grace would need more and more support from me as time went on. It might make things easier in the short term, but someday, she would need constant care, not my divided attention. I proposed the idea that I take a leave of absence from work in order to spend more time with Grace, assuring myself that I could give up work if I needed to, but Peter knew me better and refused to accept that I would be happy living that way. I felt palpable relief when he rejected the suggestion. "That's not a solution, Connie," he had replied, eyeing me candidly. "We both know you couldn't be happy like that." He was right, and I was relieved that he knew me so well. So we kept looking. What we needed was a solution that would adapt with her. I hesitated because I was afraid of what these changes would mean for me. Up until now, knowing that I could manage Grace's Alzheimer's disease was reassuring. It made me feel like I had control over the situation. Admitting that I couldn't manage Grace's needs made the shadow of the disease more frightening. Peter and I talked about it, weighing the pros and cons, circling around the fact that Grace needed more daily support. Something had to change.

Peter and I discussed assisted living; Peter knew the contractor responsible for a new facility near our house, and after reviewing the building plans and the cost, we had agreed that it might be the right option. We discussed buying two attached rooms so that Grace could have overnight guests, which might ease the transition. We discussed it with her, emphasizing that this move would allow her to keep her independence while still having the option of help if she needed it, and though she wasn't convinced, she accepted my suggestion to go and see the individual units that had already been constructed. The building was still about a year from being ready, so there was very little pressure on her to accept an immediate change, but I tried to excite her about meeting the other people who had already bought units in the complex. I didn't mention Alzheimer's disease and neither did she. She would admit that sometimes she couldn't remember things— she referred to her medications as "for her memory" but rejected the diagnosis aggressively. She wouldn't accept that those words could ever apply to her. Dr. Gaede told me that having Grace accept the term was less important than having her accept the changes that the disease dictated. And so, I booked a tour.

I maintained a cheerful tone as we drove down to see the suites in the new facility. We could have walked, it was so close to our house, but I wanted Grace at her best for our visit, not tired or windblown. Grace was quiet as she sat in the car beside me, but I was excited, imagining that we would both be surprised by the advantages this move might offer. When we arrived, we could see that the building itself was completed, and inside, the main floor was fully finished and decorated. There were tables set up for visitors, and an accordion player and dancer were drawing attention on one side of the room. I had been through all the details with the facility director earlier in the week, so I repeated what I knew to Grace as we looked around. Grace nodded as I spoke, but she gripped her purse tightly in her hands. It was clear that she wasn't happy here, but I suggested that she sit down while I go and check on the suites. I hoped that while I was gone, she would try a little harder to see the advantages of this place. She didn't watch me as I walked to the back of the room, but I could see that one hand had come off her purse and was hovering around her chest, which told me she felt particularly anxious. After a few minutes, someone wheeled an older man to the table, and I hoped they would strike up a conversation. One of the staff stopped at their table to offer a plate of cookies, and from a distance, I imagined that Grace was softening under all this attention.

I stood at the back of the room for almost thirty minutes, wanting to give Grace a chance to think about living in this place, but she didn't talk to the man with her at the table. She just sat and stared around the room with her hand clutched at her chest. I circled around the room before I started back toward the table, and as I got closer to Grace, I could see the pinched expression on her face. After a beat, Grace lifted her head and shot me a withering look, her face contoured by scorn. As I sat down beside her and looked across the table, I understood why. The man she was sitting with was leaning heavily on one arm, his eyes staring vacantly out over the garden. His hair was smoothed down on top but stuck out at angles around his ears. His mouth was slightly open, and the sides of his lips were wet with spit. He didn't react to my arrival at all. For a moment, I felt unsure of what to do. This place didn't feel like an acceptable solution anymore. I wanted Grace to live in a place that would support her and help her to feel capable. I wanted to push back against the disease, but here, that support would be coupled with a vision of her future with this disease. I didn't want Grace to become complacent, surrounded by silent, staring people. I didn't want Grace to think of herself as old and sick.

The air in my chest escaped out of me quietly and took with it my enthusiasm. The look on Grace's face confirmed that we weren't ready for this place yet. I reached for Grace's hand and said lightly, "I think we should go. Are you ready?"

Without hesitation, Grace said, "Yes." We walked to the car and drove home in silence. I didn't know what to say about what we had seen, but I knew that something had to change. And I needed to admit that to Grace. When we got back to Grace's condo, she opened the door and walked straight over to a photo of Bob on the wall and said, "They are killing me, Bob. They are killing me! If they think I can live there . . ." I tried to interject, to say that I knew it wasn't the right place, that we would find a different solution, but she ignored me. After a moment, she wheeled around and spoke passionately. "Don't make me go there. I'll crawl under the sink and drink the bleach! I can't live there!" and then turned back to Bob's picture, no doubt hating the fact that he wasn't here to help her. I felt torn, knowing that I couldn't keep going as things were but not wanting to condemn Grace to unhappiness. I pulled her to the couch and talked to her for an hour, trying to convey my dilemma. She was full of uncertainly, afraid that she couldn't trust me, and her hands played with the buttons on her shirt as she tried to keep herself calm.

Eventually, I tried to reason with her. "We need some extra help Grace. We can't keep going, just the two of us. We need to find someone who can give you a little extra help when I can't. I don't want to make you move if you don't want to, but we do need to make some changes. I need to you agree to that, okay?"

There was a long pause before Grace looked up at me. "Yes," she said quietly. "Yes, I agree."

I squeezed her hand then and kissed it, wanting to reassure her that we were a team, that I was only searching for a way to make her life easier.

I had no clear idea of what to expect from a caregiver; I only knew that Grace needed someone who would help her with small tasks and errands and keep her calm when she got riled up. For several days after visiting the seniors' home, I daydreamed about how our lives would improve if I could find a caregiver for Grace. I imagined this person becoming a genuine friend to Grace, someone who would love her and care for her like I did. I wanted this person to smooth over the rough edges of Grace's daily experience and help me to understand how to respond to the developing disease. I reasoned that this person would become part of the family—I pictured all of us seated together around our table on birthdays, our faces bright with candlelight; I saw myself sharing winking looks with this person as Grace mixed up the details of her day. In my mind, it would be like an Alzheimer's disease version of *Who's the Boss*, with me as Angela and this caregiver as Tony, working together to overcome the comic misadventures of Grace's memory. It was calming to think about this caregiver and the confidence that they would give me.

I had gotten used to living with the vague but constant worry that Grace was somehow at risk when she wasn't with me, but that feeling disappeared when I imagined life with a caregiver. "How could Grace not be safe with a professional?" I asked myself, feeling almost gleeful. She would be safe and happy and bubbling over with stories when I went to see her each day. And with everything taken care of, I could be more focused at work and more relaxed at home. Ultimately, I could be a better friend for Grace when I wasn't drained from also trying to be her guardian, pharmacist, nurse, and parent. Peter and I had talked about it at length before I started looking in earnest. He was happy with the idea of a caregiver not only to relieve my stress but also his own. He knew how to smooth over Grace's moments of confusion, but he worried about the future, when she would need more personal help: getting dressed, going to the bathroom. He couldn't imagine being so intimate with his mother; as her son, there was an invisible line he didn't want to have to cross. Part of me wanted to wave away his concerns and assure him that he would be fine, that he and Grace would muddle through, but I didn't, knowing how much the idea stressed him. I could understand his hesitation, and I didn't want to fuel his fear by pressing him. He didn't like to talk about what it would be like when Grace needed significant care, and so we focused on the present, on finding a caregiver for Grace. Peter and I assured one another that the caregiver would help us answer these more difficult questions.

Imagining the help a caregiver could offer us spurred me to action: I called Pamela to tell her about my plan, and then I sat down and wrote out an ad to place in the local paper. I titled the ad "Fun but Forgetful Mother," and in it, I explained that Grace needed a companion who could do some light housework and help her with meals. I described a companion who would take Grace shopping and on little day trips and might have dinner with us in the evenings. I wanted to convey my hope that Grace's companion would become part of the family. Writing these things out, I felt confident that they would wing their way to the right person. I submitted the ad to the paper and fell into bed thinking that Grace and I would soon have an ally. As I drifted to sleep, I felt confident that I was ready for the phone to ring.

The phone did ring the next day at 7:00 a.m., and when I reached for it, bleary-eyed, I assumed it would be Grace. What I didn't assume is that it would be a job applicant. I launched out of bed and toward my office, a tiny nervous knot forming in my stomach. I had nothing prepared for this call—not formally anyway. It had been on my list of things to do, but I thought it would take a few days to get a response. The voice on the other end introduced herself—Margarita—and I heard the words *companion* and *mother* as I shuffled papers, distracted by my wish for some sort of checklist to guide me through this conversation. The voice was musical; the woman spoke quickly but her words seemed to curl up at the ends so that the last syllable of every word landed softly. With only a few prompts, she covered her training and experience, sharing fragments of stories about past patients with deft confidence and occasional laughter. I soon stopped trying to capture anything with my pen and just listened as she narrated stories of people like me and like Grace. I felt entranced by her, speaking so easily about how she helped her other clients, bringing order to their lives. Suddenly, help didn't seem so far away, and it occurred to me that, if I hired her, I wouldn't be alone anymore. It was an overwhelming feeling.

Margarita asked questions, looking for specifics about what we needed, and with a flash of nervousness, I began talking, telling Margarita about my Grace. I knew I needed to stay focused on the practical requirements, but I also wanted to make sure she understood Grace's personality, her kindness, and the need to be circumspect about the disease itself when she was around. "She needs company, mostly, and someone to be available to help her do things that she shouldn't do alone, like errands. I don't want her to feel like she is being monitored," I explained, wondering if others had ever said the same thing to Margarita. Did caregivers often have to disguise their roles like this? The question threw me off, but Margarita took it in stride, explaining that it was common enough and that it was no problem, especially in the beginning. Relieved, I listened to her talk about ways past patients had responded to news of a caregiver. I didn't know exactly what else I needed to say, and so at the next pause, I suggested that we meet and go from there. Margarita offered time that afternoon, but I postponed for two days, wanting time to plan the meeting more thoroughly. I gave her my address and took her phone number, and we said good-bye, her accent a charming echo in my mind.

I was left with the impression that Margarita was confident, warm, and chatty—she seemed like just the kind of person Grace would get along with. It nagged at me that I didn't really know what questions to be asking, that I didn't have any firm sense of Margarita's training or expectations of me were, but I pushed these doubts off. She was certainly motivated, and that made an impression on me. I needed someone with a lot of energy, someone who could recharge me with their confidence. As I sat at my desk, I let myself think of what a difference it would make to have Margarita on my side, helping me with Grace. A smile crossed my face as I pictured the three of us chatting easily, and Margarita explaining to me the little tricks of managing Grace that would make life easier. It was easy to imagine these scenes of victory, all loosely based on the stories Margarita had told me during our call. These scenes stayed with me most of the morning.

There were lots of other phone calls over the next few days, so many that I stopped keeping count. I think, by the end of the week, there had been more than one hundred different calls. After the first few, I got into a routine of asking questions that would suss out essential information like qualifications, experience, and long-term interest. The voices on the other end of the phone were always different: some were loud and forceful, and others were meek; some were native English speakers, and others could barely understand me. It was overwhelming, and I was underprepared. I had imagined getting three or four calls from expert caregivers, not being inundated with questions from so many strangers. Many of the callers explained that they needed work permits, and while I dutifully wrote this down, I didn't really understand what this meant. The sheer pace of the calls put pressure on me because I wasn't really prepared to evaluate so many people so quickly. The disparity between the strongest and weakest calls worried me because I wasn't sure that I could pick out the best person from the growing group of applicants. It seemed silly to feel out of my depth as I'd hired and fired employees at my company for years and had always felt confident in my ability to select the right person for each job. I didn't like to admit that, when it came to hiring someone for Grace, I was less sure what I needed and what made someone the right choice. I booked appointments with a few of the people who seemed to have the most experience and ignored the nervous feeling in my gut.

Margarita's interview was my first, and it went well. She knocked on the door exactly on time and shook my hand firmly as she came in the door. Her accent, Chilean, she explained, was softer than it had seemed over the phone, and I liked the way it sounded, warm and confident at the same time. She chatted easily about all the concerns I raised about Grace and nodded knowingly when I explained that I didn't want Grace to know that she had a caregiver. I wanted to introduce the caregiver to Grace as a friend of mine and let Grace's natural hospitality take care of the rest. Margarita said that this approach had worked for past clients, and I smiled, relieved. In the end, I chose Margarita as Grace's caregiver. Of all the applicants, she seemed the most confident. She had strong feelings about diet and activity and made me feel sure that Grace would be well cared for. That and she was willing to accept a live-in position. She had two grown sons and was divorced, so moving in with Grace was ideal for her. I was glad to phone Margarita and set her employment in motion. In my mind, I was already thinking about how to introduce her to Grace.

I spent the next morning working with Grace on her little balcony garden and arranged to have Margarita come over during the afternoon. We snipped dried flowers off the plants and pulled the reaching weeds out of the soil, and when we settled back to review our work, I took a breath and told Grace a lie. In my defense, it was a small lie, intended to help Grace be . . . graceful. I wanted to inspire Grace's better nature, not her stubborn streak, when I raised the topic of the new caregiver. Dr. Gaede called them therapeutic fibs and warned me not to overthink their role in managing Grace. Grace had agreed to accept changes in her care, and we'd discussed other assisted living options since the disastrous visit to the first facility, but raising the topic of Margarita was difficult because Grace maintained that she didn't need full-time care. I had already made the decision to hire her as Grace's companion, but I didn't want Grace to feel that she had no say in the matter; I wanted to find some way for Grace to say yes and feel in control of the situation. And so I asked Grace whether she would mind helping a woman I knew who had lost her job and was struggling with finding a place to live until she could find another job. In exchange for rent, she would help clean the condo, do the shopping, and generally help out where she could. Grace was immediately invested as I expected her to be. She loved having houseguests and was always happy to help anyone in need. And Grace was so relieved to have escaped the threat of living in the facility that having Margarita stay with her seemed a welcome option. She wanted to know all about Margarita, and over lunch, she peppered me with questions, sometimes repeating the same ones with the same bright look on her face. I answered evenly and felt pleased that the stage was so well set.

When Margarita arrived at Grace's apartment later that afternoon, Grace was bubbly, excited to welcome her in and show her around. It was a relief to me to see Grace so pleased with the situation even if she didn't fully understand what Margarita's role in the house would be. Margarita played along well and paid careful attention to Grace as she spoke. After all my worry about choosing the right person, it seemed that Margarita was going to be a great fit with Grace. I left with Margarita, and we both promised Grace that we would be back later that evening with some of Margarita's things. Outside, I hugged Margarita and said good-bye and walked home feeling genuinely hopeful in a way that I hadn't in a long time.

It was Grace's good nature that let me feel confident—she was an inherently kind person, especially when she felt she could help others, and her eagerness to welcome Margarita into her life made the transition easier for all of us. It was something that I felt immediately when I first met her—welcomed, invited—and since marrying Peter, I had become familiar with all the family stories of Grace's goodwill. Her sisters told me how, when she was a teenager in Salt Lake, she would make all her own dresses and finish them with elaborate embroidered trim, sitting in the kitchen each evening to have the best light for the detailed work. Once each dress was finished, Grace would model it for her sisters, sashaying just enough to make the skirt sway and beaming from ear to ear. Her sisters would coo over Grace's work, but before they could ask to try it on themselves, Grace would offer it freely, saying, "This shade is really meant for your coloring, Colleen" or "The waist detail will show off your figure, Jean!" Knowing Grace as well as I did, I could easily imagine Grace clapping and praising her sisters as they modeled her careful work, happy to have made them happy.

Grace was always inspired to share and happiest when she was giving to other people. Her parents had always given very practical gifts at Christmas, but Grace liked to give extravagant gifts. Some of these gifts have been described to me—Jean and Colleen still remember them well—but the one that always stuck with me was Grace's first extravagant present to Jean: a pair of velvet pajamas, perfectly tailored, with delicate, fur-covered buttons up the front. Jean insisted on wearing them for most of Christmas Day, bewitched by the weight of the expensive fabric, and Grace was thrilled. It was a gift that was perfectly Grace—elegant, luxurious, and something Jean would never have bought herself. Grace believed in living richly, if only in small ways, and it was a lesson she impressed on her family at every opportunity. Grace liked gifts that made others feel confident and beautiful. It was one of the reasons that her store had done so well, and it was the reason that she welcomed Margarita with so much charm. When it was in her power to help people, Grace was motivated to do whatever she could.

It was hard for me to gauge how involved to be with Grace and Margarita as they settled in together. Margarita reported back to me each day, so I knew that she and Grace were getting along and that Grace had someone close by at all times. Peter and I had them over for dinner a few times as well, and everything seemed to be progressing nicely. It wasn't until a few weeks later that Grace called me with a concern, and in the pause before she began to speak, I felt familiar tension creep up my back. Grace's voice spilled down the line "You know, your friend spends an awful lot of time with me—I don't need as much help as she wants to give me." It wasn't accusing, but it felt that way to me, like I had failed to instruct Margarita on how to play her two roles at once. I feigned surprise and laughed it off, but once I hung up with Grace, I resolved to ask Margarita to be less intrusive in Grace's life. Grace still liked her independence and her routine. She liked to get up in the morning and have a cup of coffee while she read the paper before getting dressed. She didn't like being interrupted or rushed through this routine but was too polite to say so to Margarita, who appeared at the table, dressed and chatty, each morning. I spoke to Margarita the next day and explained that she didn't need to be so involved in Grace's day and that, so long as she was monitoring Grace and was available to help when necessary, that was enough for now. It was a small tweak and seemed to improve the situation.

We fell into a routine; most nights, when I got home from work, I would walk over to Grace's house to pick her up for dinner, inviting

Margarita or leaving her free for the evening. Some nights, I would call Grace and have her meet me halfway between our two homes. If I had our yellow lab, Sasha, with me, she would tug on the leash as soon as Grace rounded the corner that separated us. Because I trusted her on our quiet street, I would unclip the leash and watch her bound her way over to Grace's slim frame. Grace would always bend down to say hello to Sasha and then look up at me with a beaming smile on her face. It is one of my favorite memories of that time in our lives, when Grace was still strong enough to walk on her own and Sasha was still alive, her heavy tail thumping against my leg as it wagged. We would walk back to the house arm in arm, Sasha ahead of us, trading small details about our days.

Knowing that Grace had Margarita to help her let me be more focused at work and made these daily reunions more pleasant because I could trust there wouldn't be any unexpected fires for me to put out. Grace seemed happier too; she would tell me about Margarita's day as well as her own, and it was nice to hear how their lives were blending together. It wasn't until I heard it happening that I realized that I had had one very specific expectation for Margarita—I wanted her to be with Grace long term. I wanted Margarita to become part of our family and to be a reliable friend to Grace as the disease developed and took her farther from us. Margarita was a source of stability to Grace, and that was something I needed to nurture and protect. I didn't want Grace to ever reach for Margarita and find that she was no longer there. It felt like a fair trade: I would take responsibility for keeping Margarita happy so long as Margarita kept Grace happy. Happy and safe. It was a different kind of balancing act, but it felt more achievable for me, at least in the beginning.

More than seeing Grace happy, I was relieved to be able to rely on Margarita's knowledge and experience with Alzheimer's patients. Margarita's training had impressed on her the importance of cleanliness and good nutrition, and she was fastidious about Grace's diet. I had accepted that nothing would reverse the disease, but keeping Grace in good health was part of my mantra about keeping her safe—safe from anything that would compromise her daily comfort. Margarita was proactive about Grace's care and made suggestions about minor improvements that we could make in Grace's life. She offered to take Grace to medical appointments so that I wouldn't have to leave work, and while I initially refused, feeling that I couldn't miss these discussions with Grace's doctor, I did invite Margarita to come along and offer her insights on Grace's health. After a few of these group visits, reassured by Margarita's ability to raise concerns and discuss strategies, I started to book appointments for just the two of them. They were still written in my day planner, but slowly, I learned to trust that Margarita had everything in hand. In part, I had to break my habit of claiming control over everything in Grace's life, and Margarita helped me to do that. She stemmed the chaotic tide of Grace's Alzheimer's disease so that the waters of my own life were less choppy.

I watched her with Grace and never saw her exhibit the stress that I sometimes felt when Grace would lose her place and repeat herself or become angry without reason. I knew, logically, that it was partly because, when I cared for Grace, other responsibilities were still on my mind; I could rarely focus on Grace alone. Margarita took away that pressure to manage Grace and work and life, all at once; she let me focus on one thing at a time, and for that, I was grateful. I was relieved. I could run in all the directions I needed to, always with the confidence that Grace was fine. It was exactly what I had been hoping for when I first admitted that I couldn't do it all myself, and yet, it wasn't as comforting as I imagined it would be. It was unsettling to feel that Margarita could provide better care for Grace than I could. I felt a sense of guilt as Margarita became expert at managing Grace's needs, a nagging sense that maybe I should have found a way to continue that balancing act or that I should have left my job to be the one to care for Grace. I felt guilty about the relief I felt at not being the only one responsible for managing the disease and smoothing the wrinkles that it created in Grace's life.

I often felt that I had been given a choice between Grace and myself, and I had chosen myself instead of Grace. That feeling was a weight that never left me, even when my logical brain insisted that hiring Margarita was the best solution for us all. It is a feeling that persists years later, although time has reassured me that I made the right decision in admitting that I couldn't do it all alone. I couldn't have been Grace's only caregiver without compromising my sense of fulfilment, without growing bitter at the cost of self-sacrifice. I would've come to blame the disease for too much and perhaps lost sight of Grace along the way. Ultimately, I've accepted my feelings of guilt as the cost of a good decision. I've realized that the guilt I feel doesn't mean that hiring a caregiver was the wrong decision; it was one option among many, and all decisions have a cost. Our lives are more stable for having outside help. The real struggle was admitting that I needed help, that I couldn't do it on my own. The real effort was realizing that what I could give Grace was enough even if it wasn't everything.

Chapter Six

The Value of Fallibility

Fallibility can feel like a threat. It undermines surety. Fallibility is the risk that we narrate around when we map our plans and goals. It is something we ignore as we aspire to the ideal. Of course, we know that we are fallible, but sometimes, we are surprised by our errors, our mistakes in judgment, our bad choices. We don't like to trace out the ways that our mistakes have hurt others. We work hard to avoid errors, and once we've made them, we work harder to cover them. Failing publicly is harder than failing privately. And so we aspire to thwart the sense of shame that accompanies failure. I don't like admitting fallibility, even to myself. I don't like admitting that I'm not sure of the way forward. I don't want to diminish the feeling of security and confidence that others hopefully feel around me. I want to be the leader who handles doubt privately so that the rest can follow with confidence, and so I've learned to smile and cheer while masking my own concerns. I've learned to hide my fallibility whenever I can, to make others feel safe. And when everything falls apart, I am the first to try to pick others up and reassure them again. Disguising fallibility is a constant process.

What I didn't consider is that sometimes the feeling that something is wrong is a warning, not a threat. Sometimes, admitting a mistake is the most important and valuable thing we can do, and to hide from that is to create more chaos, not less. Understanding that we are fallible should also come with the understanding that we have the capacity to fix our errors and make things better.

***

Margarita stayed with us for five years, and in that time, she helped us come to terms with some significant changes in Grace's ability and behavior as the disease progressed. She spent birthdays and holidays with us, moved back and forth between houses with Grace, and became a fixture in our lives. It was hard to remember what life was like before she was with us and impossible to imagine what life would be like without her. She and Grace were close, and when I was with them, I saw an easy back and forth that made me glad that I had asked for help.

One of the advantages of Margarita was her availability. The fact that she was divorced and her two sons were fully grown meant she was available to travel with Grace to Palm Desert each winter. Although it got harder to organize that trip as Grace's Alzheimer's disease developed, I was determined to maintain her routine. Without Margarita, it would have been impossible; even with Margarita's help, it was difficult. I gave Margarita one week off every month regardless of where Grace resided, which meant that I flew down to Palm Desert every few weeks to give Margarita a break, and I organized my work schedule accordingly. When I was in Palm Desert, I spent my days with Grace and my early mornings and late nights with my computer, trying to stay on top of everything back home. I loved my time with Grace, and being able to maintain our routine felt like proof that the disease hadn't yet started to limit Grace's freedom. So I kept up the trips and the cross-country marathons that Grace and I had been doing together for years. As they got harder, I worked harder to keep Grace relaxed, to contain the confusion and frustration that rose more quickly as the years passed. In that, Margarita was my ally.

Not that there weren't some problems. Perhaps if I had been really looking, I might have seen them more clearly. But I wasn't looking. More importantly, the most serious issue was one that did not appear at first, only presenting itself as my relationship with Margarita evolved. Like so many things in life, the problem emerged so slowly that I didn't really comprehend how much things had shifted until some time later. While I was initially glad to let Margarita take charge of Grace's care, I began to feel that I didn't have a good handle on what was happening with Grace. Because I spent less time with her, her Alzheimer's disease symptoms seemed more noticeable. Seeing the disease expand to claim more of Grace was difficult, and my increased concern about her began to cause some strain in my relationship with Margarita. At that time, I would have said that the problem was me. When I hired Margarita, I considered her an expert; I relied on her to show me how to best care for Grace. All I wanted was for Grace to be happy; that was the only provision I made about her care. I let Margarita take it from there. When she handled Grace the way I would have, I felt reassured that my instincts were correct and that I had found the right solution for Grace. But when she did things I didn't understand, when I didn't agree with her actions, I didn't question her. I didn't want to insult her or seem ungrateful for her work. She and Grace had become friends, and I didn't want to risk disrupting Grace's life by upsetting Margarita. If Margarita decided to leave, all our stability would disappear. And I loved the space Margarita cleared in my life for my work. I loved knowing that I wouldn't be getting frantic phone calls from Grace while I was at the office. I loved being able to focus on growing the company again rather than treading water so that I could be available for Grace. Ultimately, I needed Margarita to care for Grace more than I needed to get along with Margarita. And so I ignored the problems that were growing between us.

When I hired Margarita, I was hiring her for the long term. I wanted her to become a friend and family member; I wanted her to feel at home with us and with Grace. I encouraged her to raise any concerns with me, and I tried to eliminate the formalities of employment between us. I gave her a credit card to make purchases for Grace and I provided her with a car so that she could take Grace on errands and day trips. I wanted her to feel that she was trusted and respected, expecting that her loyalty and affection would be gifted to Grace. When I got home each night, I'd ask Margarita about the day, and she would answer with one of the endless variations of "Today was fine. Grace was in a good mood." I was always relieved to hear a positive report, but it was hard for me to get a full picture of how they spent their days together, and I didn't want to seem like I was checking up on them. So I would nod and say that I was glad. Sometimes Grace seemed tired or irritated, and then, I didn't know how to reconcile Margarita's report with what I observed. But I said nothing, deferring to Margarita's judgment.

Because I didn't spend as much time with Grace, I didn't have any sense of Grace's daily moods, her eating habits, her bouts of confusion and anger; it was not as easy to track trends or foresee problems. For a long time, I rationalized that handing over control meant I couldn't be on top of everything, but I always resented the disadvantage of knowing only what Margarita would report each evening. It wasn't until a year or two later, when I hired an additional caregiver on a part-time basis to give Margarita more time off, that I realized how much I was missing. The new caregiver suggested that we keep a logbook of Grace's days, recording her sleep, meals, bowel movements, meds, moods, and any outbursts. She explained that short-term trends would make it easier to anticipate long-term changes in Grace's abilities and health. It made so much sense when I thought about it that I felt concerned that Margarita hadn't suggested it herself. In that moment, I stopped assuming that Margarita was infallible. That day, I went out and purchased a big leather-bound notebook and wrote up a list of all the things I wanted to know about Grace's day-to-day care. When I explained my expectations to Margarita, I brought the care manual with me to show her that it was a recommended practice for Alzheimer's disease patients. At first, she resisted, but after a few false starts, she fell into the habit of taking notes about Grace's days and I read through the book each night, glad for the window into Grace's experiences. Having that record let me see patterns in Grace's behavior, so I felt more sure of myself when I was with her. It took a long time for me to realize that I had to be clear about what I expected from Margarita. I had assumed that good communication would just flow, that both parties understood what was needed in this regard. I ended up learning the hard way that communication or lack thereof was a major problem.

One of the reasons I tried to make Margarita think of us as family was to reduce her hesitation about calling us if there were problems. It was something I repeated to her often. I wanted to be sure that, when I didn't hear from her, I could safely assume that everything was fine. She didn't call often, but she called when she needed to, and I felt confident when I traveled for work that Margarita would keep me informed and in touch with Grace. I bought her a cell phone so that she could always reach me. When I was away from home, I always kept my phone with me, wanting to be available for either of them. As Peter rationalized, the whole point of a caregiver was to be there when Grace needed her, and, until one fateful afternoon, Margarita had always shown herself capable of managing Grace.

Peter and I decided to spend the weekend out on the West Coast, just to get away. We did some sailing in the harbor, enjoying the salty air. It was midafternoon and we were debating dinner when my cell phone rang. I recognized the Calgary area code but not the number. I held the phone up to my ear, hoping that it wasn't a call center. There were office noises in the background, and I sighed, thinking that I should have let it go to voice mail, when a man spoke, asking my name in an official, questioning voice. He identified himself as a Calgary police officer, and when I heard those words, I felt a torrent of electricity race through me and felt a momentary collapse before my fear caught up with me and propped me up. "Yes, Connie Ruben, yes," I answered, wanting to hurry him along. I could hear him shuffle through pages and then he said Grace's name and my heart dropped, even though my mind couldn't understand what he could be saying.

"Grace seems to have . . . wandered off," he said, "and you are her emergency contact, correct?"

I was stuck on the words *wandered off* and couldn't understand what he was saying. "What do you mean, wandered off? Wandered where?" was the only response I could manage, and I had the impulse to hang up and call Margarita, who would surely tell me that Grace was napping or sitting on the balcony with her flowers. But I clenched the phone as the officer explained that Margarita had reported Grace missing to the police office about an hour earlier.

I could hear myself breathing heavily into the phone as the explanation followed: Margarita had driven Grace to our house, just a block away, and left Grace in the car while she went into our garden to water the plants. When she came back, the car was empty and Grace was gone although her purse was still sitting on the floor of the car. The officer assured me that everyone was out looking for Grace and that she would be found quickly. All I could hear was that Grace was missing, without identification. "Surely she recognized the neighborhood and went straight home," I suggested to the officer, but he explained that Grace's apartment had already been checked, and she wasn't anywhere near her building. He had no other information, but he promised to call us as soon as they found Grace. Then he hung up, leaving me panicked over Grace and angry that Margarita hadn't called me immediately after she had called the police. I'd said the words "Just call me" to her hundreds of times; I'd said them just before I'd kissed Grace's cheek and left for the flight out to Vancouver yesterday. Why hadn't she called?

I paced the room and alternated between holding back tears and growling in frustration at Peter. This wouldn't have happened if I'd stayed in town, I thought to myself, hating that I'd felt so confident about leaving. I considered calling Margarita, but what was the point? I needed her looking, not explaining. All these thoughts circled around me until, not long after the first call, I got a second call from the same number, and the same officer came back on the line to say that Grace had been found and that she was fine. He didn't have all the details, but apparently Grace had gotten bored waiting for Margarita and got out of the car, thinking to walk home, but had gotten confused at the corner, turned the wrong way, and gotten lost. She'd wandered into a hair salon in the neighborhood, looking lost enough to prompt someone to stop and ask her if she was okay. The image made my eyes sting. She hadn't been able to remember my name or Peter's or Margarita's, but she knew Alberta Mining, which was the name of the family company. It was the only thing she was sure of, and so the person called the police, asking for someone they could contact, and eventually, the police called the company number, reaching the answering machine recording, which listed my cell phone in case of an emergency.

It was a relief to know that she was safe but I couldn't forget that in a crisis, Margarita hadn't called me. When we discussed it later, she apologized and explained that she didn't think I could help, being out of the province, but I knew that she hadn't called because she didn't want to admit her mistake, afraid of getting into trouble. After that, I realized that I needed to be firmer about what had to happen in emergencies, and in nonemergencies too. It was a hard situation to recover from; I was angry at Margarita for not calling, but that anger wasn't helpful. I knew that losing track of Grace could just as easily have happened to me. Her error was in not informing me, hoping instead to resolve the crisis without me being aware of what had happened. For a long time after that, I couldn't trust Margarita the way I had before, and I couldn't trust myself either. As a follow-up, I got Grace a "safely home" bracelet, which links to a database with all her information so that, if she ever gets lost again, whoever finds her can contact me immediately. Though it gives me comfort to see it around her wrist, a part of me still worries about her when she is away from me.

That day changed my relationship with Margarita. I no longer saw her as the expert in elder care and myself as the neophyte thrown into an unfamiliar world. I knew from that point that I needed to play a bigger role in Grace's life. This desire, however, met with some resistance from Margarita. Over the years, she had become comfortably ensconced as not just Grace's caregiver but also as head of the household. My early deferral to her expertise had given her a sense of empowerment that made it difficult to feel that we were really a team. And although I didn't like to admit it, I had played a role in creating the problem. I covered for her when she asked for time off, always wanting to be accommodating and keep her happy. At first, this meant an extra day off over a weekend or getting home early so that she could leave for the evening, and I managed her requests by juggling my own schedule. But over time, Margarita started to take advantage of my commitment to Grace by giving less notice and asking for more time off. She once announced that she needed a few days off, starting the next day, and left me scrambling to move meetings at work so that I could be home with Grace. She seemed to see my schedule as flexible even though it never felt that way to me, and increasingly, she would assume that I would make myself available to cover for her. This situation was even more complicated when she and Grace were down in Palm Desert. The first time she called me from Palm Desert to say she needed unscheduled time off, I felt trapped. I couldn't just leave work and fly down without notice, and Pamela couldn't help either, but Margarita was insistent that I find a solution. Flustered and under pressure, I proposed that we hire a second caregiver who could stay with Grace and give Margarita more time off, but Margarita didn't like the idea of sharing responsibility on a permanent basis and warned me that two caregivers might be more stressful for Grace. I backed down and booked a flight to Palm Desert a few days later, giving Margarita a week's holiday. In my mind, it was what I had to do to ensure that Grace was properly taken care of. And after that, it began to feel like I was on-call, ready to jump in when Margarita needed me to. It was a frustrating situation, but I accepted it because my goal was to keep Grace comfortable.

I knew that Margarita wielded a great deal of power in our house and Grace's, but it wasn't until we reached an impasse over a change in living arrangements that I realized just how imbalanced the relationship had become. This arose from my attempt to solve a complicated problem. The daily routine that connected Grace with Peter and me—our dinners together—were becoming difficult to manage again. Nights when I didn't leave the office on time, I had two options. The first was to rush through dinner with Grace so that I could still have her in bed on schedule. Inevitably, I would eye the clock on the stove while I ran back and forth, trying to organize the meal while maintaining a fragmented conversation with Grace and Peter. When I was late bringing Grace home and Margarita was waiting, I'd tense inwardly and wish I'd taken option two. Option two was less stressful and more at the same time. I could always cancel dinner and have Grace eat with Margarita, but I hated making that call. Grace's voice on the phone was always slightly unsure, and the lift that came when she recognized me would dip again as she repeated my words: "No dinner tonight." I couldn't help feeling in those moments that my life had squeezed Grace out, leaving the both of us disappointed. When Peter and I were eating alone, I'd feel guilty that I had chosen work overtime with Grace. After months of battling these two options, it occurred to me that we should make a change.

I turned over the problem in my mind for a long time, but I couldn't see any way to really change the situation. The anxiety of rushing between our two homes after work was stressful. Another important part of the puzzle was that I wanted to have a better insight into how Grace was doing and how Margarita was interacting with her. As close as our two homes were geographically, they were still two different worlds.

How could I solve this? I turned the puzzle over again, trying to reason a way forward. It might have made sense for Grace and Margarita to come and live with us. We had room to spare and if Grace were here, there would be no running between homes. This thought faded as I imagined Grace in our house. She was here often enough but rarely went up or downstairs. It wasn't reasonable to have her sleep upstairs when getting down to the main floor presented such a challenge. And the move itself would be difficult on her; she'd been in her condo for years, long before Bob died, and losing the comfort of that space could stress her. Her memory was slipping daily, and I didn't want her to have to confront a new world every time she woke up. I couldn't find a solution that didn't displace Grace, and I couldn't let myself do that. The only other solution was for us to move in with Grace, which seemed like an outrageous suggestion until I really sat down and thought about it. It would be a significant adjustment for us all, but it was the easiest way to keep Grace comfortable, and her condo was big enough that we could make it work. It was an unlikely suggestion, but simple enough to work.

At first, Peter resisted. Although he loved Grace, he was concerned that we would lose privacy and space for our own relationship and that I would feel even more responsible for Grace if we were living together. I waved his concerns away, but we both knew that what he said was true. It was a major decision for us. We discussed it for a few days, talking about how we could reconfigure her condo so that we each had private space at opposite ends but shared the common space in the middle. The more time passed, the more I was sure that this was the best solution for all of us. Once I explained my vision, it wasn't hard to convince Peter, though he had quirky perspective on the idea. He didn't like to think of himself as a grown man moving back in with his mother, so he suggested we buy the condo from her so that, instead, she would be moving in with us. I wasn't sure how much he was joking and how much he was serious, but that became the plan.

I was anxious to tell Grace all about our plan, but before I did, I sat down with Margarita to get her thoughts. The change would affect her life as much as Grace's, and as I thought of her as family, I wanted to consider her feelings as well. She didn't hesitate at all. "It's good, it's good that Grace will have you close by," she said, nodding agreeably and patting my hand. I was thrilled and hugged Margarita before rushing off to explain things to Grace.

When I talked to her, I left out the financial details and simply explained that Peter and I wanted to live with her so that we could have breakfast and dinner together each day. "Oh," she said, looking surprised, speaking slowly. "Are we having dinner together now? I'd like to change . . . will it be a party?"

I laughed at this and put my arm around Grace's shoulder so that I could still see her sweet face waiting for my response. "Yes, Grace, I think we should have a party! We'll call Peter and make sure he'll come, and then we should get into the kitchen and see what we can whip up!" Grace beamed at the promise of a project together. She didn't cook anymore, but she liked to hold the measuring spoons for me while I poured in oil and vinegar and whatever else was called for. As we cooked together that afternoon, I felt calm, not rushed at all. And I felt confident that this plan would improve everything.

The next few months were a blur; my days were connected by lists of things to organize: Realtors, bankers, contractors, designers. The sign in front of our house went up quickly, and I had boxes delivered to the house so that we could start packing away what we didn't need. All we were waiting for was for an offer on our house, and even that came relatively quickly. I got the call from our real estate company one afternoon with an offer, a real one. I was ecstatic. I called Peter on his cell and caught him between meetings to relay the details of the offer. After Peter, I called Margarita, wanting to tell her and Grace the news. I waited impatiently for the phone to ring, and when Margarita answered, I started into my story, ending triumphantly with the announcement that the house would soon be sold and that Peter and I would be moving into the condo. I was anticipating Margarita's response, anxious to get home to explain it all to Grace in person. But no response came.

"Margarita?" I asked, unsure.

But then Margarita's voice boomed over the line, strong, even angry. "If you sell your house and move in with us in the condo, I'll quit!" And then, silence.

For a moment, neither of us took a breath at all, and I turned her tone over in my mind, as it said more than her words did. Where was this coming from, I wondered, flabbergasted. What did this mean? Was she serious? I stumbled off the phone, trying to sound calm, promising that we would discuss it tonight. I should have been angry. I should have been indignant—I'd given her the chance to raise concerns, to say she didn't like the plan, and she'd said nothing. In fact, she claimed she supported it. But I couldn't let myself be mad. I held my emotions back because I was afraid. Afraid that, if I pushed her, if I moved forward regardless, she really would leave. I was afraid to be alone, Grace's sole caregiver once again. More than that, I was afraid to disrupt Grace's life since Margarita had become such a major fixture in it. All I could think was that I needed to maintain this situation and that I couldn't risk making demands on Margarita. I could either sell our house and throw everything else into chaos or take the house off the market and retain stability in Grace's life.

The conversation with Margarita that night was just as unproductive as the phone call had been. She would only say that she didn't want to live with her boss, that she didn't want to be watched all the time. I tried to reason with her, explaining that nothing was really going to change, that this was only to make it easier for us all to take care of Grace. I promised more time off, rationalizing that I could clear my schedule more easily with Grace in the next room. But Margarita was adamant. She would leave if we proceeded with this plan. Inwardly, I was enraged, but I felt I needed Margarita so much that I couldn't afford to lose her. For days, we sat on the offer to buy our house, asking for more time, all the while trying to find a compromise that would tempt Margarita from her intractable position, but there was nothing I could offer her.

What made the situation impossible was that it was soon time for Grace's yearly migration to Palm Desert. She and Margarita were set to leave within weeks, and I needed Margarita on that plane with Grace. How could I confidently hire someone local and send them to Palm Desert for six months on such short notice? And anyone I hired in Palm Desert would be unlikely to want to travel back to Calgary for six months each year, which meant that Grace would be shuffled between multiple caregivers until we got her back to Calgary. She was attached to Margarita and happy with her routine, and I didn't want to force disruption on her.

I was completely unsure of which way to turn. I had never felt so uncertain, so fallible, with respect to knowing how to best care for Grace's interests. As the days passed and the man who made the offer began to press for an answer, I lost my nerve and convinced Peter that we needed to take the house off the market. We refused the offer and I watched as the real estate agent pulled the sign up from our lawn, frustrated but unsure what I should have done differently.

I had a lot of time to think about that question while we were in California. With Grace and Margarita in Palm Desert while Peter and I worked from San Francisco, where we kept a houseboat, I considered the corner Margarita had backed me into and vacillated between bitterness and disbelief in my own weakness. Why hadn't I challenged her? Why had I capitulated like that? As I signed Margarita's paychecks, I had to remind myself that I was her employer and not the other way around. I felt like I had no control. I'd let my gratitude toward Margarita and my guilt over not caring for Grace myself turn me into someone I didn't recognize. I remembered Dr. Gaede telling me that, if I didn't take care of myself, I wasn't taking care of Grace, and suddenly, seeing the situation between Margarita and myself clearly for the first time, I knew that I needed to reclaim control. Things were neutral between us when we were all together down with Grace in Palm Desert, but in my heart I felt that a line had been crossed, and I could not forget that.

I kept in touch with the Realtor, and as Grace's time in California drew to a close, I told him to put our house back on the market. Then I sat down with Margarita. For the first time, I approached the meeting like an employer, and I explained to her in a firm tone that Peter and I were moving into the condo with Grace, and that, if she didn't like it, she could give her notice. I was resolved to the possibility that she would quit. Despite the fear of transition, I needed to remind myself that she wasn't irreplaceable; perhaps a change might even be a good thing. I kept all this to myself while Margarita and I spoke, but it must have been written on my face, because she assured me that she had no intention of leaving or interrupting the sale of our house. It was infuriating to hear her say that after her point-blank refusal months earlier, but I simply nodded, thanked her, and left the table. It felt good to be firm, even just a little. It was long overdue.

The house sold within a few months, and soon after we moved into the condo. Peter made jokes to Grace that he was moving back in with his mother in his old age, and she would smile and pat him on the arm. Moving into the condo with Grace was, for many reasons, the right decision, but the battle of wills that had taken place between Margarita and me raised some uncomfortable questions: Why had I given her so much power over me? Why was she still dictating what she did and when? They were simple questions, but the answers were complicated.

I'd lost sight of why I'd hired Margarita in the first place. I wanted Grace to be safe and cared for, and the feeling that I couldn't do it alone made me overly grateful for the help that Margarita offered. I took her help like a life preserver because I felt intimidated by the disease that peeked through Grace's eyes each day. And I felt guilt too, for choosing to keep working, for not quitting my job to care for Grace. Perversely, that guilt made me feel like I shouldn't expect to be too happy, that I should take some lumps for choosing to go with a caregiver for Grace rather than filling that role myself. I felt indebted to Margarita for giving me freedom and bowed to her expertise because I doubted my own ability to fully care for Grace. This began a process of empowerment for Margarita that created an unhealthy imbalance between us. Even when I became aware of this fact, I felt trapped into accepting what had become the pattern of our relationship.

Somewhere along the way, I realized the error in my thinking. Paying Margarita to help Grace wasn't me shirking responsibility; it was me demonstrating responsibility for Grace as well as for myself. I needed help for Grace, but I needed help that wouldn't come at such a cost. I also needed to have more confidence in my own instincts and abilities with respect to Grace's care. I may not be a trained or certified caregiver, but I had some important advantages. I knew Grace, and I loved her. Through the years, I had come to know Grace intimately enough to know what she wanted even when she wouldn't ask it for herself. I knew what made her happy and what caused her discomfort. These were the fundamentals of good caregiving.

I needed to let go of the guilt and the insecurity and start taking control. It was a difficult step for me. I wanted to do the best for Grace, whatever that meant, but I needed to recognize that there would be times that there may not be a very clear path. I needed to accept fallibility and to let go of the fear that I would not always do the "right" thing. Kicking myself over the wrong choice—well, I just didn't have time for that. I said these words to myself for a long time before I felt confident enough to act on them. It was soon after that that I realized I was not doing a service to any of us by keeping Margarita on. The time had come to end the relationship before it got worse. Taking the time to realize the problem gave me the encouragement I needed to make the tough decision. I felt a sense of calm that I hadn't had in a long time. I felt clearheaded and ready to make changes in Grace's life and my own. I realized that the dynamics of my relationship with Margarita had become unhealthy for Grace and for me. I'd let my sense of need confuse me and given Margarita too much power. And so I decided to let Margarita go.

As sure as I was of the decision, it certainly was not an easy conversation to have. Margarita had been with us for a long time, and though she knew there were problems between us, she was surprised by my decision. I reassured her that Peter and I would provide a nice severance package and we would make the car part of the package as she did not have one of her own. Though I was ready to part ways with Margarita, I had no desire to hurt her. I knew that she loved Grace and that in itself meant a lot to me.

When I got home that evening, after firing Margarita, Grace was sitting on the couch in the living room, running her finger along the stem of a bright red tulip from the vase beside her. With the door shut, I sat down beside Grace, confident in myself for the first time in a long time. Grace pulled the tulip out of the vase and held it toward me, her face curled up in an elaborate question: "Is it just us two ladies then?"

I laughed, tickled by Grace's spot-on analysis of the situation, although she did not yet know that Margarita would not be coming back. "It is, Grace. Just the two of us," I replied, and Grace smiled, turning the flower back toward her face so that she could smell spring in its red cup.

"Good," she sighed, "we should have a party."

Being without Margarita was not as scary as I'd assumed it would be; caring for Grace alone was actually easier than having a caregiver who would disappear without warning and send my world into temporary tailspins. I had been afraid to let go of the support that I thought Margarita provided, but when I did, I could suddenly see my situation with Grace very clearly, and I knew what I needed to do. This time, I wasn't going to screen a hundred phone calls; this time, I was going to find a professional, and I was going to interview them like any other employee. Gone was the idea that all I needed was another family member; now I knew I needed reliable professional care for Grace.

The change was also beneficial from another aspect. The level of caregiving required had escalated as Grace's Alzheimer's disease had progressed. When Margarita was hired, I was still hiding from that fact a little, still wanting to see Margarita as a mother's helper instead of a caregiver. Now, I had no such illusions. Grace needed full-time care. She couldn't be rushed or spoken to aggressively. She needed to be reminded to eat, to go to the bathroom. She needed a patient listener who would wait as she pulled the thin threads of her memories into a story. Six years after her diagnosis, I finally had a clear vision of how to manage the chaos of Grace's mind. I needed to let go of my idea of creating companionship around Grace and instead surround her with people who could keep her safe and happy. Safe first, then happy.

I wrote out a list of the responsibilities expected from a new caregiver and a breakdown of Grace's daily routine. It was empowering. I was finished negotiating, and finished bending to the priorities of others. This time, Grace's needs were first; but mine were second. If I was going to pay for care, it would be the care Grace deserved but without any drama or battles between me and the caregiver. I had my expectations with me during interviews and decided to hire two caregivers instead of relying on one. Two caregivers would give Grace more consistency and avoid the kind of scheduling problems that had become increasingly common with Margarita. The process of hiring was much easier this time because I felt in control. I was making a business decision rather than searching for a friend. I was in my element, finally.

Having some distance from the process of hiring made it easier to make decisions. I was direct about my expectations, I listened for caregivers to use words like *support* and *enable*, and I watched Grace carefully when she was introduced to prospective caregivers, still wanting someone who would be caring and chatty with Grace.

My first hire was a woman named Ruth, who impressed me in her interview and won an easy smile from Grace. Then I hired a relief caregiver named Joyce, who worked evenings so that Ruth had enough time off. I still had to be on my guard to make sure that I didn't fall back into my old behavior of trusting the wisdom of the paid caregiver even when I knew it to be incorrect. I needed to remember that the person I needed to trust the most was myself simply because I truly knew Grace. Though I might not always have the right answer, I needed to make my expectations for Grace's care understood.

My newfound resolve and confidence was quickly challenged. Ruth called me from Palm Desert one day, explaining that Grace seemed to have a chest cold and should be taken to the emergency room. I certainly was not a doctor, but I did know the ER was the last place I wanted Grace to be, unless there were no other options. The anxiety of sitting in a room of other people for what could be hours would put a significant strain on Grace. I asked Ruth to wait while I arranged some alternative. I phoned the doctor at a local walk-in clinic who had treated Grace in the past, and when I explained the situation, he agreed to see Grace right away. When I phoned the house to explain it all to Ruth, no one answered. Not wanting to believe what my gut was telling me, I phoned Ruth's cell phone number. Ruth answered and told me she and Grace were on their way to the hospital. She reminded me that I had hired her to take care of Grace and that I should trust her to do so. I was speechless for just a moment, shocked at being disregarded so openly. Then very calmly, I told her to turn the car around and take Grace to the walk-in clinic where the doctor was waiting for her. I explained that, if the doctor believed Grace needed to go to the emergency room, then that would be our next step, but it was not going to be the first step. It was not until I hung up that I realized my hands were shaking. I'm sure it was partly because I was upset at Ruth for so flagrantly ignoring my instructions, but partly it was because I had gone against the advice of the caregiver. What if I was wrong and the solution I had arranged was not the best one? What if my decision had adverse consequences for Grace? But even with these doubts in my mind, I felt sure that my solution was the best one. I knew Grace well enough to know the impact of a long wait in an emergency room would have on her. I had to trust myself. It was a reminder that I needed to stay involved in not just the hiring of the caregiver but in the guidance and direction of the care itself.

After this incident, I had serious doubts about Ruth and, sure enough, the coup de grâce came during a phone conversation just a few days later. Ruth casually mentioned that she had hidden the large vase of artificial flowers that were on the dining room table. She explained that she had removed them because Grace was constantly going on about how beautiful they were and it was frustrating to listen to Grace's fixated chatter. I could not believe my ears. If I could have reached my arm through the telephone line, I'm sure my hand would have been around her throat. These flowers were a focal point for Grace as she sat at the table each day working on her jigsaw puzzle. She would comment on how beautiful they were because they were a source of joy to her. Yes, her comments were repetitive and constant, but that is a symptom of a short memory cycle. Some people are not meant to work with Alzheimer's disease patients, and Ruth was clearly such a person.

I called Regina, the director of the local care service who had introduced me to our second caregiver, Joyce, and explained what Ruth had done. Regina didn't miss a beat; she called Joyce to start work early and both of them went over to Grace's Palm Desert house. When Regina arrived, she asked Joyce to take Grace into the bedroom and then called me from the house phone, putting me on speaker with Ruth. Skipping all niceties, I addressed Ruth. "Please pack your bags right now. I don't want you in my house. Regina will take over from here."

Regina said she would take care of everything from that point on, and she did. She turned out to be one of the most important allies I would ever have in dealing with Grace's Alzheimer's disease. She was a care consultant, and after Ruth was fired, she sat me down and explained that as the employer, I needed to enforce my own rules and give clear guidelines for Grace's care. She groaned when I explained that I had given Margarita her own credit card and let her have Grace's car, shaking her head gently as I narrated my desire to provide for the caregiver so that she could provide for Grace. "But that's not how this works, Connie. Someone needs to be in charge, and that has to be you. You have to manage the caregiver while they manage Grace." And hearing it from her, it made total sense. Her calm, matter-of-fact tone connected with me and gave me confidence. I realized that what she said was true, and it laid the foundation for a much healthier relationship with future caregivers.

Joyce became Grace's primary caregiver in Palm Desert, and she and Grace formed a friendship, which centered around conversation. Joyce would sit with Grace and listen to her stories. She would ask Grace questions, prompting Grace to retell the stories that she still remembered. They would eat breakfast while sitting in the sun and then go for a drive so that Grace could admire the flowers carefully cultivated in the green lawns of Palm Desert. Joyce would take Grace shopping, walking slowly through the air-conditioned mall so that Grace didn't get tired. Besides being a gentle and attentive caregiver, Joyce was also a trained nurse, which I could see was needed for this next phase of Grace's life.

For the next couple of years, Joyce managed Grace's care while she was in Palm Desert and I used a local care agency, Home Care Assistance, to find caregivers in Calgary. After so many missteps in finding the right kind of care for Grace, I have learned a great deal. When I look back, I can understand some of Margarita's concern about living with us. At times, it has been difficult to have Grace, the caregivers, Peter, and me all under one roof. The need for healthy professional boundaries and clear communication is imperative. Although it requires more compromise, the advantages of having Grace with us trump the inconveniences. Each evening when I get home, I spend a few minutes with Grace in her end of the condo before I tell her that I'm going to check on Peter. She always thanks me for coming by and encourages me to come visit again. The fact that I only have to walk a few feet to what we call "the other side" of the condo means nothing to her but the world to me. I have a structure in place that allows me time for myself as well as Grace. The caregiver assumes she is to feed Grace unless I call her during the day to advise otherwise. This way, I know I don't have to rush away from the office and that, when I do get home, I can enjoy my time with Grace.

But the greatest advantage of having Grace with us is hearing her laughter. We have the privilege of having a group of caregivers these days who go above and beyond being attentive to Grace's needs. When Grace is relaxed, they will watch television together; although Grace cannot follow along, she is happy to have them sit and hold her hand as they enjoy the show. Most nights though, Grace needs more interaction in the evening, and our caregivers, Alvi, Maya and Meylenne, whom we collectively call the ladies, have discovered Grace's favorite entertainment: karaoke. Grace doesn't sing anymore, but the smile on her face when others sing to her is unmistakable. It fills my heart with joy to hear the ladies performing jubilantly for Grace as they laugh and hold her hand. Peter and I often join in the fun, and Grace will slap her hand on the edge of the sofa, keeping the beat of the music while the rest of us sing to her.

Other nights, I listen as the ladies read to Grace. Several years ago, I wrote Grace's story. I started with her early childhood and took it through her later years. I didn't know at that time what a treasure that story would become for her. She listens endlessly to the story of her life: sometimes, she will remember the events that I've described in the story and add details of her own; other times, she asks repeatedly whom the story is about. I am so thankful for the caregivers in our life today. The quality of their care flows from a true love in their hearts for the woman they call Madam Grace. They are a blessing and I know how fortunate we are to finally have arrived at this place. They are comfortable with the fact that I am the authority in decisions about Grace's care, but our interaction is easy, collaborative, trusting, and respectful. Grace is in the care of loving hands, and that knowledge gives me a sense of peace and contentment.

Chapter Seven

The Pleasure of Acceptance

Getting to a point of acceptance sounds like getting to a destination. It sounds like the place we arrive at the end of a journey full of suffering. It seems to promise the end of hardship. But acceptance isn't an endpoint, a static achievement. Acceptance comes when we learn to balance reality and our desires, when we find a way to accommodate both without losing ourselves. For that reason, acceptance is dynamic, always in flux. Learning to live with change creates acceptance.

Control is an illusion. Regardless of the chaos in our lives, we never stop trying to impart our own sense of order on the world. The result is always imperfect. The task is beyond our ability. The goal is flawed. And when we relinquish control, we can discover something more valuable: the strength to accommodate change without breaking. It is natural to fight chaos. I fought Grace's Alzheimer's disease for almost ten years, and though there were illusionary moments of reprieve, in truth, I never won a single battle. I can't even imagine what that victory would look like. When I fight the disease, I am fighting an enemy who feeds on my fear and frustration. I am fighting an enemy who never gets tired. When I fight, I hurt myself and Grace. There is no way around that. For a long time, I thought that fighting the disease would keep me close to Grace. I thought it would let me hold on to her more securely. I was wrong.

I've made peace with Grace's Alzheimer's disease. I've learned to look past it, to see Grace first instead of the disease. And that has made all the difference to our relationship. Accepting the chaos of her world has given me the freedom to laugh instead of cry, to see humor instead of defeat. My time with Grace is different now. We move together in a smaller circle, but there is more laughter now that I'm not so afraid. Now that I'm not focused only on what I've lost, I can see more clearly what I still have and what I've gained in the exchange.

***

Learning how to stand up for Grace taught me to be strong when Grace lashed out at me. It is a difficult thing to see her confusion give way to rage, to see her thin body shake and her eyes narrow at me, untrusting. She is usually calm and mild-mannered, but when her memory disappears for more than a few minutes, she becomes defensive and aggressive. When it first happened, I knelt beside her and said my name over and over in a calm voice, trying to give her something to latch onto so that her memory would return. There were times, later, when that didn't work. Sometimes her anger would catch light, and there was nothing I could do but keep her safe until she ran out of fuel. When I watched this demonstration, I'd feel my own anger and panic rising up to meet hers, and I'd want to scream and cry as well. It was desperation, not knowing what to do, not knowing how to reason with Grace. Each time it happened, I tried to step away from the scene in front of me; I reminded myself that I was seeing a moment of the disease, not a vision of the future. But it scared me just the same. I didn't know how to respond.

A few years ago, Grace and I were in Vancouver together. I had already planned a business trip when the caregiver asked for a few days off. The easiest solution was to bring Grace with me, up to the Sunshine Coast. The flight was just over an hour, which was still inside Grace's comfort zone, and she was in a good mood when we landed, which cheered me. I tried to think about this trip as a vacation for Grace, and being in Vancouver, I'd arranged for her to spend some time with Rob's two teenage sons, Solomon and Josiah. I reserved a hotel room with a big living room so that we could eat in the room rather than going out for dinner. Avoiding crowds helped Grace to be relaxed, and the strain of travel required that I make some considerations. I had meetings planned for the first two days, to which I could bring Grace. On the third day, Grace's grandchildren came over to visit, and we went for a walk in Stanley Park, down by the waterfront. Grace was in her walker, and for once, it took no convincing to get her to use it. The boys walked with her around the gardens and helped her to maneuver around the crowds and through it all, Grace grinned and laughed, thrilled with the boys' company.

We went back to the hotel midafternoon and ordered pizzas for dinner while we played card games, which was still one of Grace's favorite activities. Every so often, Grace would look over at the boys and say, "It's so nice that you've come to visit us here. It's just lovely!" Each time she said this, she'd nod at me, asking if I was pleased as well. Then she would play her turn, placing her cards down deftly, and smiling up at us all. Watching her made me smile to myself, amazed that she could move so quickly between confusion and cleverness. Her good mood made me glad that I'd arranged this trip for her. Sometimes these things were a good idea; sometimes they were a mistake. This time, it seemed worth the extra effort. We were having such a good time that I didn't realize how late it was, and though Grace seemed fine, I suggested that Grace needed to get to bed. The boys kissed Grace gently and praised her extravagantly before leaving, and once they were gone, she settled back on the couch, chattering happily about the day we'd had. Inside the room, I began listening to the phone messages that had piled up while we were out.

As I listened, writing names and numbers into my day planner, I watched Grace. She was looking out the living room window toward the city lights, content, although her face seemed tired. Her eyes were fixed on the distance, and every so often, she'd comment about something beyond the window, pointing into the dark. I was surprised that she wanted to stay up as it was 10:00 p.m., which was late for her, but traveling tended to disrupt her normal routine, and I was happy to have company as I reviewed the agenda for tomorrow's meetings. It felt a little bit like sitting in our own living room together after dinner, and I felt relieved that the trip had been so successful so far. Moments like this let me feel that the disease had released its grip of her a little, giving us the chance for small adventures. I stood up, heading for the bedroom to get my laptop so that I could review the documents the office had sent. On the way back to the living room, I stepped into Grace's room and put the rest of Grace's clothes into the dresser—she didn't like living out of a suitcase—and turned on the lights so that, when I brought Grace in, it wouldn't be dark. Settling the room relaxed me because I knew it would relax Grace.

I heard Grace from the living room, talking loudly. As I walked toward the door, her voice got louder, her tone frustrated. "Grace," I called, walking down the hall toward her. "Grace?" She wasn't answering me, although she was still speaking as if she was talking to someone in the room. When I rounded the corner, Grace was standing between the couches, her arms lifted up toward her chest, her hands folded one inside the other. Sleep was gone from her face, replaced by worry; her eyebrows knit together while her eyes darted around the room.

"I've lost the baby. I think, I put the baby . . . ? Did I leave it at home? I did. I left the baby . . ." Grace's hands squeezed each other tightly as she chattered, her thoughts escaping her mind incomplete.

I stepped toward her slowly, not wanting to agitate her. "Grace? Grace? Everything is okay, Grace. The baby is safe." It was common, this worry. When this happens—I call it an Alzheimer's fit—she fixates on early memories. She talks about being at home and making the baby safe. I still don't know whether this is a real memory about her own babies when they were young or if this is just a generic worry that she just can't let go of, but in the moment, I knew all I could do was be calm and assure her that she and the baby were safe.

I moved toward her slowly, speaking easily, trying to avoid asking questions. Questions only stressed her. "I'm going home now!" she announced, looking between the window and the door, then directly at me. "I'm going home. I want to be at home. The baby is at home, all alone. I have to go." Her tone was strong until the last syllable, when her voice cracked and faltered, making her seem more frightened than angry.

I was only a few steps from her, but I knew I needed to settle her down before I came too close. I sat on the couch and patted the seat beside me, looking at her evenly. "Grace, let's sit down. The baby is safe and so are you. Sit."

She ignored me, staring again at the door, her arms still folded across her chest. Her voice cracked again as she spoke. "I have to go home! Now!" She stormed back, away from me, and then behind the couch. It was that movement that made me feel the first surge of panic. Usually, when Grace was like this, she would still respond to me. Usually, my voice would calm her down, not rile her up. This felt . . . different. I stood up, turning toward Grace. She was standing between the bedroom hallway and the door, facing away from me, as if she was trying to decide which way to go. I tried again, saying her name calmly. She didn't move. Again, panic. This wasn't normal for her; this not responding.

The silence was broken by our breathing, both of us panting a little from the stress in the room. "No!" Grace shouted toward the wall. "I'm leaving, I have to be at home now, with the baby. It's my baby!" She turned toward the door, and though her hands were still clutching her chest, I lunged toward the door, not wanting to let her leave the room. In a few steps, my body was blocking the doorknob, my arms raised, ready to embrace her, ready to hold her back. All the time, my feeling of panic grew: What was I supposed to do? What did this mean—was this happening because she was tired? Was this the start of a new phase of the disease? What if she didn't relent?

Grace didn't want to be near me, so she backed away from the door. She continued fighting me, demanding to be let out, demanding that she be taken home. All the time, her eyes didn't leave the door. I double-checked all the locks were in place, then stepped away for a moment, reaching for the table beside the door where I had dropped my purse and the key cards to the room. I slid the table loudly in front of the door, wanting to bar Grace's exit more definitely. I wanted to put a limit on this moment, not wanting it to escape past me into the hall. For a brief second, I thought about taking Grace's hand and leading her out of this room, downstairs and outside. Maybe being outside would calm her down? But maybe it wouldn't. Maybe on the street, surrounded by strangers, she'd scream more loudly and try to get away from me, turn away toward traffic? The scene played itself out in front of my eyes, ending with the shrill sound of car brakes, and I felt my body press more firmly against table in front of the wall. I couldn't risk taking her outside. I would have far less control there.

Grace's sharp cry underlined my decision, jaggedly demanding my attention. "Take me home! Home! HOME!" Her eyes were like mine, full of panic and confusion. I felt trapped in that room, unsure of how to deal with Grace. My frustration welled up, tipped with fear. She wasn't responding to me at all; nothing I said seemed to make a difference. She wasn't hearing me. All I could think was that I needed to distract her somehow. Her mouth opened again, ready to challenge me, and the sight of Grace broke me a little: her eyes bulging, her fists drawn over her chest, her feet stamping with all the energy she could muster for this battle. I was still trying to form a plan when Grace rushed toward me, her jaws snapping, trying to bite me. In her mind, she was fighting for the life of her child. I was so shocked that all I could think to do was step out of her way for a second so that I could wrap my arms around her chest from behind. I felt her resist me, felt her small fingers pinching my arm, and once she realized that I was dragging her, she began to shout again. She had no words, but she shouted anyway, enraged at being denied. With her back pressed against me, I started down the hallway toward the bathroom. Grace's legs quit, refusing to help me, and within a few steps, I was dragging her.

The bathroom door was open and I flicked the light on with my shoulder. I didn't really have a plan; I was just making it up on the spur of the moment as, both of us fully dressed, I pulled Grace's fighting body into the shower with me. With one hand, I fumbled with the faucet, struggling with Grace as I listened impatiently for the sound of the water to divert up into the showerhead. When the water started to spray out, drenching us, we flinched at the cold temperature, both panting at the effort that it took to get us here. I said nothing, and neither did Grace, and my arms continued to hold her firmly, although I could tell almost immediately that the fight had gone out of her. We stood for a few minutes, both of us feeling our clothes grow heavier. I was afraid to speak, afraid that Grace would start again with anger, but when I whispered her name, her reply was calm. I released her then, and she turned to me, the shower still spraying above us. "Oh, are we done?" she asked me in a steady voice.

I answered, "Yes, I think we should go to bed now," as I wiped water away from her face.

"Yes, I'm tired," she replied.

I turned off the water and stepped out first so that I could hand Grace a towel. I helped her get undressed and wrapped her up in a towel before wrapping another one around her hair. Her face was calm, the stress of our fight forgotten, or so I hoped. While I got her ready for bed, I talked steadily and she responded. "Tomorrow, I'd like to see more flowers," she said, her eyes drooping toward sleep.

"Of course, Grace," I replied, patting her hands and turning out the light on the table beside her.

"Goodnight, Connie," her voice trilled, and she squeezed my hand before patting it gently.

I stood up and walked back into the bathroom, pulling off my own soaked clothes and wishing I could strip away the gut-churning worry I felt. Wrapped in a towel, I looked into the bathroom mirror, seeing the fight reenacted in front of me. Grace's anger had scared me because I hadn't known how to deal with it or what it meant. Once again, the disease had taken me by surprise, and I felt unprepared. I hated that feeling. But what could have prepared me for this kind of scene? I peeked in on Grace on my way to the living room and she was asleep, breathing steadily. Thank God. I went to my bag and pulled out small crinkled balls of tinfoil, which I dropped along the hallway between Grace's room and the door. It was a habit I'd gotten into at some point when Grace started wandering at night: if Grace woke up and tried to leave her room, the noise of her feet against the tinfoil would wake me. But even that precaution didn't sooth my fears. What if, what if—that was all I could think. The question cannibalized the past and then the future: What if she woke in the night? What if she got angry like that when we were in public? What would I do then? What if this was my fault? What if I handled this badly? All these and more swirled around my head and I cried because I had no answers and because I knew that there would not be answers ever. Just guesses—that's all I ever got from this disease. This was just one more unresolved worry I would have to accept. All I could do was try to mitigate her stress.

The next morning, Grace work up later than usual, but though I watched carefully, I could see nothing different about her. We spent the day in Vancouver and flew home the next day, and Grace breezed through it all without any trouble. I convinced myself that our fight wasn't proof of a new stage in the disease. I decided that it was the result of too many people and too much activity, and these were things I could control. I had to expect less from her and not trust her to tell me what she could handle. I needed to watch her more carefully and think more critically about what she needed. It was a relief to think that by being watchful I could adapt to the situation. Being more aware of Grace's needs was a small price to pay for keeping her safe and happy. It was both a recognition and an acceptance that there was a new reality that we all needed to inhabit.

Moments where I see myself losing ground with Grace's disease occur more frequently now. She is easily confused, more likely to draw a blank in the middle of a conversation. She asks the same questions more often. I accept it. Her world is more fragile, more easily disrupted. I need to maintain confidence for the both of us. Usually, it takes only a few seconds to pull her back from confusion, and then her eyes light up for a moment as she recognizes me and she pats me on the hand, unaware that she's been gone. Sometimes, though, it takes a lot longer to find her again. Sometimes she is gone for hours, and then, I always feel my panic rising, afraid that this time, she won't make it back to me.

The first time it happened, not long ago, I was at work and the caregiver called in tears, announcing abruptly that Grace's memory was gone, that she didn't recognize anything. None of the usual cues were working on her. The caregiver's voice was strained under the news, and her emotion scared me more than anything. I came home immediately, trying hard to remind myself that these blank moments are expected, that she's always recovered in the past. At the back of my mind, propelling me home midday, was the explanation Dr. Gaede had given me about these moments, that Alzheimer's disease doesn't progress in a linear way, that the damage can suddenly appear after long periods without change. The fear that Grace's memory of her world might be fully gone was terrible, and it took a massive effort not to let fear run wild in my head.

When I got in the door, Grace and the caregiver were seated at the table by the window, and so I sat down beside Grace and waited for her to notice me. When she looked up, I smiled and said hello. "Do you know who I am?" I asked, willing her to smile widely and say yes.

But she was quiet, thinking about the question, and then she replied, "No, I don't."

My heart wanted to fall already, but I'd seen this before and refused to panic yet. "I'm Connie, your daughter-in-law," I offered, taking her hand in mine.

Grace smiled broadly now and responded in a relaxed tone. "Do I have a daughter-in-law?" She looked over at the caregiver and then beyond, out the window, unperturbed by our crowd of anxious faces.

I didn't want to give the impression that something was wrong, but usually Grace could tell when she wasn't remembering something, and this time, she didn't seem to mind at all. I eased away from the table and called Peter, asking him to come home. Then I clapped my hands and called Sasha, our dog, who appeared sleepily from the bedroom. It was something that had worked before when Grace's memory had disappeared; there was something about the dog that she connected with. I guess it was the tactility, the way Sasha sniffed and licked at Grace's hands, trying to have her ears scratched. I told Peter to be calm when he got here, and he knew from the tone in my voice that this was different than usual. I turned back to Grace without panic. Panic would bring me nothing; it would only scare Grace. So on the outside, I was calm.

I sat again and started chatting easily about the view from the window and about Sasha and Peter coming over. Grace was easy enough to talk to, but it was clear that she was running off of a very basic program. She would respond to questions, though sometimes only after prompting, and she was polite but distant. It felt similar to the way I would talk with a stranger while traveling. She was talking to pass the time, not saying anything particularly important. While we chatted, worry battered the door at the back of my mind. This is what it will be like someday, making conversation with a stranger, I thought. I tried to push the thought out of my head but it lingered, distracting me from everything that Grace couldn't remember.

When Peter arrived, he approached his mother carefully, introducing himself slowly and watching as Grace stroked Sasha, who dropped her golden head in Grace's lap as Grace played with her ears. "Such a lovely dog," Grace commented, smiling. We were all silent, waiting for her next words. "Is she your dog?" Grace asked, looking at Peter. She didn't wait for an answer but turned back to Sasha, who had dropped down to the floor and flipped over so that Grace would rub her belly. I mouthed the words "breakfast—eggs and toast" at the caregiver as she got up from the table, and Peter sat down, his jaw tightening as he watched Grace. I could feel the collective tension in the room mounting, so I started chattering about the dog, trying to keep Grace talking. From the table, I could hear the sounds of cooking, and it reminded me of something I'd read, a link between dementia and low blood sugar. I couldn't remember exactly what the connection was, but it did make me think that maybe we had another card to play.

When the caregiver returned with a full breakfast for Grace—eggs, toast, juice—we sat quietly, trading comments that required no response because we wanted Grace to focus on eating. She offered toast politely to us all, noting that we weren't eating with her, which made me laugh. It was typical of Grace to remember her manners even when she couldn't remember her company. Peter put on a pot of coffee and poured a cup for each of us, giving us something to do while we waited. I put on Frank Sinatra, thinking that the music might help to unstick Grace's memory. Grace finished her breakfast but none of us pushed away from table, afraid that, if we tested Grace again, we'd still be disappointed. So we chatted, trying to be enthusiastic while waiting for Grace to come back. After we had all finished our coffees and looked pensively at one another, I tried again. "Grace? How are you doing?" I asked.

Grace looked up at me and smiled. "I think I ate too much. Quite enough at least!" she replied, and then looked down at the dog, still lolling on the floor. "Sasha," she crooned, slapping her thighs to get the dog's attention. We held our breath, not wanting to push Grace. "Maybe we can take her for a walk, Peter?" she continued, looking from Peter through the window to the grass beneath.

"Sure," Peter responded, and I could hear the relief in his voice. I felt tears well just below the surface, then retreat as the fear that Grace wouldn't return ebbed away. The memory of that moment, however, didn't fade.

There was no way to know what had caused such a prolonged memory failure or to know what had brought her back. Dr. Gaede explained that these things were different for every person and that all we could do was try different ways to bring her back. "Each time it happens, you'll get better at knowing how to deal with it. And the calmer you are, the better it will be for Grace," he'd explained. In a way, it was like an inoculation, helping prepare me to accept the moment when Grace wouldn't be able to recognize me at all.

I ran through the list of things we had tried that day, trying to make sure that I wouldn't forget anything next time. I could never be sure about what was going to work, but Grace had responded to something. I could only hope that I would be able to find the right trigger the next time this happened. Privately, I worried that one day, Grace would disappear and nothing would bring her back. Had Peter said this to me, I would have hugged him and reminded him that all we could do was be glad that Grace was still here. But somehow, I couldn't manage that kind of enthusiasm for myself. When Grace turned to me and invited me on the walk as well, I felt some of my fear shift, making room for hope again. I called the office and told them that I would be late back to work so that I could take that walk with Grace and Peter. Because I knew that one day, I wouldn't have that option, and I didn't want to miss it now.

As Grace's Alzheimer's disease develops, I feel myself resisting. I catch myself pushing back against the limits that creep closer around Grace each day. In part, I don't want to capitulate and admit defeat; I don't want to accept Grace's limitations before I absolutely have to. It is in my nature to push myself, and to stop Grace from sliding away from me, I push her too, sometimes unfairly. Last year, while planning Grace's trip to Palm Desert for the winter, I decided to make a stopover in Phoenix so that Grace could spend the afternoon with her sister Colleen. In my mind, it was a quick stop: off the plane, into town, a little lunch, and back to the airport for an evening flight to Palm Desert. In my mind, it was a small price to pay to give them some time together. They don't see much of each other anymore. Now that Grace has such a hard time moving around. I feel responsible for making sure that I do what I can to keep Grace surrounded by loving faces. So I booked the trip and felt proud of my plan. It was a short flight from Calgary to Phoenix, but Grace was agitated and confused, and by the time we got out of the airport, I was starting to worry that maybe the stopover wasn't the best thing for her. That maybe I'd been pushing for this visit because it felt like something I should do more than because it was good for Grace. It was a feeling that has followed me for years now, this weighing and balancing of her need against my perception of her need, her family's needs, and my own needs. But I pushed the worry aside and focused on Grace, talking calmly in a low voice until we got to Colleen's place.

For me, the reunion was worth it. Colleen rushed at Grace with her arms out, smiling broadly, and Grace's impeccable manners prompted her to raise her arms too and smile at her sister. And after a minute, Grace seemed to recognize her, and the tension went out of her shoulders then. Lunch was relaxed, for the most part. We sat out on Colleen's patio and chatted, and Grace was as gracious as she ever was, listening more than talking, but nodding her assent as the discussion developed. And all the while, I felt pleased that I'd thought to make this happen, that even though I may have pushed Grace to come here, here she was having a good time. We stayed for four hours, and then Colleen drove us back to the airport in time for our flight.

Grace's mood started to dip when we got back into the car, agitated by the break in her routine and the unfamiliar location. I kept up a stream of chatter with Colleen to cover the change as I didn't want anything to mar the memory of this successful visit. At the airport, I pulled our bags from the trunk and hugged Colleen quickly, watching Grace carefully. Crowds and noise were stressful for her, so checking in for the flight wasn't always easy. But Grace was calm and hugged Colleen gently before whispering good-bye. I wished I had a camera in that moment, to remember the two of them together, although we'd taken lots of photos over lunch. It was partly that I could mark down the trip as a success now that I had Grace back at the airport. I felt it was a good decision and worth the strain of breaking up our trip. Colleen released Grace and hopped back in her car, and then it was just Grace and me, standing on the sidewalk in front of the big glass doors, waving into the distance. I leaned forward to take the handles for the two bags and waited until Grace adjusted her purse strap.

"That was a great visit, wasn't it, Grace?" I asked, feeling happy but relieved that the second half of our trip could now begin.

"Yes," Grace replied, looking in the direction that Colleen's car had traveled, "it was good." And then there was a pause, and Grace turned to me. "Nice people. Who were they?"

Her words hung in the air as I closed my eyes. I didn't want Grace to see how much her question hurt me. No, not hurt me. I wasn't hurt. But her question made all the effort, all the work, seem pointless. Colleen was gone less than a minute and already Grace didn't remember seeing her. Was it worth it then, to bring Grace to Colleen? If there was no memory of it, does the moment even exist? If the joy it brought her didn't last at all, is it worth the extra effort? In that moment, I felt something had been stolen from me as well.

I could still feel the strain of it in my shoulders as I pushed back against these questions. The easy answer felt so discouraging. I didn't want to accept that my efforts to keep Grace connected to the world were swallowed so easily by the disease. But I couldn't say any of this to Grace, so I held it back and answered her question evenly. "That was your sister Colleen. We stopped here in Phoenix to see her on the way to Palm Desert." Grace smiled politely at me, nodding and offering me a careful "Oh." I waited a moment for a signal that she had made the connection between my words and her afternoon with Colleen, but there was nothing. And so we turned toward the airport doors, her delicate hand in mine, as I swallowed the disappointment of knowing that I could never keep up with this disease that stole Grace's pleasures.

As Grace's memory becomes more and more tentative, the questions have haunted me: what good were visits and family experiences if Grace couldn't remember them? If, when they were over, all that was left was the fatigue in Grace's face, the strain in her eye? I wonder who I'm doing this work for, and if it is really in Grace's best interest. I have come to accept the fact that there is no right answer. I've resolved to try to make Grace happy in the moment. As her days become more fragmented, I have to stop trying to bridge the gaps in her mind and accept her reality. I have to remind myself that she lives in the continuous present, that I am no longer building memories with her. All that I can give her is my attention, my affection. She is now a creature of the moment, and when I am with her, I must be the same.

Sometimes, it weighs on me, this caring that I do so continually and fail at so regularly. Sometimes Grace's confusion and constant questions are too hard to respond to, and then, I call Peter and ask him to take over for me. It has taken a long time for me to be able to do this. For years, I felt that walking away was itself a failure, so I would stay, privately frustrated, tearful, and afraid for the future. But now, I have learned to say to Peter, "This is yours," and walk away for a few minutes. There's no point to trying to mask my feelings. Grace can sense my stress and it worries her; it makes her more likely to ask endless questions. She is only searching for reassurance, just like me.

When Grace's memory first started to slip away, I'd panic, afraid of what it meant for the future. Those moments always made me feel as if the ground had lurched beneath me, warning shocks for a bigger quake yet to come. Things are different now. I've realized a lot about this disease in the past eight years, and maybe the biggest thing I've learned is not to tense when Grace's world shifts. Her Alzheimer's disease has frightened us, but it has also given us wonderful moments; sometimes her forgetting has meant that we all get to share the thrill with Grace as she rediscovers the same surprise she had enjoyed just moments ago. Sharing her excitement and gratitude for all things is a joy that has never faded for me. These are the moments that are most special to me, moments when I've stopped fighting the disease and just lived in Grace's world for an evening. I've lived a lot in living like Grace.

There was the Christmas before Grace's ninetieth birthday, which we spent in Sausalito on the boat. The girls came down with Peter, Grace, and I for the holiday, and the day after Christmas, one of the girls came up with the idea of an early birthday party for Grace as we wouldn't be together in March for the actual day. The four of us fussed in the kitchen, making a cake, and the girls rewrapped all of Grace's Christmas gifts so that she could open them again. When we were ready, Peter brought Grace into the living room and sat her down on the long sectional couch so that we could all settle around her. Grace's eyes were clear blue and happy, loving the attention the girls paid to her, and when I turned off the lights so that we could bring in the cake and sing "Happy Birthday," Grace sat up tall and started to clap. "All these presents for me?" she asked as the girls lifted presents from under the coffee table and cheered, filling the moment with enthusiasm. All the presents were labeled "To GGG," which was the family shorthand for "Good Grace Grandmother," Grace's official title, which was invented by her oldest granddaughter, Chelsea, when she was four years old. Grace opened each gift slowly, not wanting to rip the paper, and her surprise at each item was genuine, although she'd opened each one the day before. Grace lingered over each gift, inspecting everything closely before declaring it "Perfect, just perfect!" It was marvelous, and while I watched, taking pictures each time Grace held something up and smiled, it occurred to me that it was a moment only possible because of the disease. The thought was bittersweet, but I was glad of it anyway. After so many difficult, frightening moments when Grace's memory disappeared and left us all uncomfortable, it was amazing to see how much fun it could be, reliving great moments with Grace again. To her, the pleasure was new and fresh, and when we accepted the world she lived in, we could be a part of that joy.

A simpler memory I have is of Grace's ninety-first birthday, which we celebrated in Palm Desert. We organized dinner at a local Italian restaurant where the waiters sang Broadway tunes—something Grace was sure to love. Music was something that she still had a memory for, and she could sing along with the old songs of her youth without missing a beat. The real surprise was that we were able to arrange for Grace's best friend Ginia from Calgary to have dinner with us. Peter went ahead to the restaurant while I helped Grace get dressed, and once Peter texted to confirm that everything was ready, Grace and I drove over to the restaurant. We walked slowly through the door, letting our eyes adjust to the dim light, and I guided Grace over to the table where Peter and Ginia were standing, waiting for us. Grace moved slowly, and I had my arm around her waist to help her navigate the tables and pointed to Peter. "I see him. That's Peter," Grace responded, and when she got close enough, she moved to embrace him.

When she released her grasp, he held her hand and gestured toward Ginia. "Look who else is here to see you, Mom." For a long moment, Grace said nothing, but her face raced from confusion to consideration to recognition.

"Ginia wanted to be here for you, Mom," I offered, wanting to supply the name in case Grace couldn't pull it up on her own.

But it wasn't necessary. Grace let out a massive breath and whispered, "Oh, my dear Ginia!" as Ginia moved around the table to hug Grace tightly. Peter and I locked eyes, praising each other silently for this idea.

Grace and Ginia sat together all night, chatting and sharing their plates as the waiters performed around them. Every so often, Grace turned to Peter or me and, forgetting that Ginia was actually there, asked about Ginia with a tone of longing, wondering how long it had been since they had seen each other. Whenever she asked this question, we listened sympathetically and agreed that it had been too long. Then we gestured to the seat beside Grace, and Grace turned to find Ginia looking back at her. Every time this happened, Grace clapped her hands together as if it were a twenty-year reunion and announced, "Oh, my dear! I'd recognize that face anywhere!" before leaning in and kissing Ginia's cheek.

I have learned to take pleasure in the little intimacies that Alzheimer's disease has created between us. Some of my most treasured memories of Grace are not moments when I have been able to see past the disease but when I have seen the disease most clearly. Mornings are my favorite time to spend with Grace, so when I can, I listen for the sounds that she is waking up and then slip into her room to chat with her for a few minutes before she gets out of bed. One morning, I crossed the room to open the drapes and then turned to her and said, "Good morning, sleeping princess," which usually makes her smile. This time, though,

I could tell from the look on her face that she was confused and lost. "You don't know where you are, do you?" I asked gently.

She shook her head. When I asked if she knew who I was, she answered, "No, but you look familiar and you have a very nice face."

I smiled and began to recite the details of her life, which was a well-practiced speech for me: "This is Palm Desert, where you live in the wintertime. In the summer, you live in Calgary. I am Connie. I am married to Peter, your son. We have three daughters, Chelsea, Lindsey, and Katie."

She watched me carefully as I explained these facts, nodding to show that she recognized each name. When I finished talking, she smiled at me and said calmly and graciously, "That is all well and good, but who am I?"

The question caught me off guard but made me smile. For all I had explained to her, I had forgotten to supply her with her own name. "Grace," I said, settling beside her on the bed. "Your name is Grace." And at that, she smiled and nodded again.

I've taken small advantage of Grace's short memory and used it to help keep her calm and happy. While I'm away, I phone her every day. Sometimes she knows it is *me*, and other times she just knows it is *Connie* on the phone. Either way, she is delighted to have the phone call. And when I'm on a business trip that will take me away from Grace for several days, I send her a greeting card each day. This way the caregiver can take her to the mailbox to check the mail, and there will be a letter there for her. It makes her happy to feel connected to me, and it makes me happy too.

Last spring, I was driving between Calgary and Palm Desert to see Grace and I stopped in Las Vegas for a girl's night on the Vegas strip with an old girlfriend of mine. While we were out, watching the spectacle of lights out in front of all the hotels, we came across a campy little store selling exuberant feather boas in all sorts of colors. They seemed just the thing for our adventure, so I bought two and we wore them everywhere we went that night. The next day, I packed them in my luggage, thinking that Grace would get a real kick out of them. When I got to Grace's house and talked to the caregiver, I grabbed the boas and went outside to surprise Grace. She knew I was coming, but I didn't expect her to remember it, and I was looking forward to seeing her face when I came through the door. That's been something I've realized about Alzheimer's disease—so often, it makes everything harder and strips the fun from events, but sometimes, it can turn everyday events into magic moments. I've learned to savor those moments. Grace loved the boas, loved that they were pink, and she wrapped herself up in them as she sat out in the sun, looking out at the grass. "Oh, Connie, they are *so* ellie-gan-tay!" she pronounced, striking a pose from her seat. We sat together and chatted, and every so often, she would swish a boa in my direction to emphasize a point. No matter what else she's lost, she still has her sense of humor. It is one thing I haven't had to let go of, and I hope I never do. It is what makes her Grace.

That afternoon, we went to the mall to drop off her broken glasses at Lens Crafters and agreed to walk around while they were being fixed. We walked slowly, arm in arm, window shopping, which Grace still loves to do. We've been shopping together for so long that we can usually pick out things for the other, and Grace loves to give fashion advice, just like she once did in her own shop. She also loves a deal; she gravitates to sales racks and looks carefully at each piece before moving past it. It can be hard to get her to try things on now because the process of changing takes a lot of energy, but I've learned to pick out things for me as well as her and then ask her if she will go into the fitting room with me, which she always agrees to.

Sometimes I'll pick up something really ugly and hold it out toward Grace and say, "Ooh, Grace, this is fantastic! I'm going to buy this for you!"

Grace, without missing a beat, will lift an eyebrow and say, "Only if you get one for yourself as well, Connie!"

Then we both laugh, and I feel incredulous that Grace is sick at all. In moments like this, there is no sign of her Alzheimer's disease, and she is just my best friend, the person who laughs easily with me.

While we were walking around that day, I convinced Grace to try on a Ralph Lauren button-up shirt, plain and white. It was simple, but Grace fingered the stitching carefully and pronounced it well made. We walked out of the changing room, Grace still in the shirt, trying to decide if she liked it or not, and wandered over to the jewelry display. She looked intently at the necklaces and eventually pulled one out and held it against her chest. "Oh, Grace," I began, and then we both chorused, "Ellie-gan-tay!" She stood back to see the necklace around her neck in the mirror, and after considering the look, she turned to me with the air of a consummate fashionista and said, "The necklace, it ups the shirt."

I nodded, laughing at the attitude of her pronouncement. In some ways, nothing had changed. We'd been having this same back and forth for almost two decades now, and she has always been wry and clever, making me laugh with her confidence. Sometimes I can't see this side of Grace, but I'm always grateful to have her in my life.

Chapter Eight

Living in the Present

One of the unacknowledged casualties of Alzheimer's disease is the ever-diminishing ability to be entertained. When I first met Grace, she was an avid reader and Peter often spoke with pride of the essays that she had written when it was her turn to review the works of famous philosophers and authors through her Great Books book club. Although Grace still loved books, I began to notice that she would start new books without ever finishing them. At first, I dismissed it, but eventually I realized that, as her attention span shortened, it became harder for her to remember plotlines or characters. Over the next few years, she stopped reading books altogether. Although she continues to leaf through the paper each day, it has reached the point where she is no longer able to parse the stories under the headlines.

The same situation occurred with movies. After Bob passed away, Grace, Peter and I got into the habit of spending our Saturday afternoons walking through the mall, window shopping, and then watch a matinee movie. It was a routine that let us enjoy each other's company, even though by the time we were home for dinner, Grace would have forgotten what movie we had seen and would swear she hadn't been seen a film in years. But over time, we found ourselves having to be more careful about picking movies that could hold her attention. Complicated plots or too much dialogue would cause Grace to grow restless in her seat. At some point, Peter and I decided that it was just too difficult for Grace to understand and enjoy movies. Although it doesn't really matter, I wish I could remember what our last movie together was just so I could fix that memory of us sitting together in the dark in my mind.

I have tried to fight back against these losses, tried to find distractions for Grace that bring her joy. I started reading to her and having the caregivers read to her as well—not published books but two books that I made specifically for Grace. After years of sharing the original Great Books series with her book club, Grace's own great books came down to just two books that I created for her. The first was a book that I made about our family; there was a page for each of Grace's children and grandchildren, and all the extended family as well, with photos and a brief explanation of how each person was related to Grace and what they were doing at this point in their lives. I had originally put it together thinking it could be useful as a reference for Grace, but as her memory has faded away, her love of this book has grown, and she can happily spend hours looking through the images and hearing the descriptions of each person. The second book I created is full of short stories written by members of the family, including Grace's sisters. I asked everyone to write about their favorite memories of Grace, thinking that it was important for us all to remember Grace as she was. But it is Grace who loves those stories best because they are the stories of her life: of growing up in a small company coal town in Utah, getting her first job, traveling to San Francisco, becoming a wife and mother. As her cognitive powers have dimmed, we sometimes have to remind her that she is the person at the heart of each story, but generally the stories are familiar enough to keep her enthralled.

My real challenge, though, has been finding ways to let Grace entertain herself. Fortunately, there is one activity that has been a mainstay for Grace right through to this day: puzzles. When I first met Grace, she loved doing the *NY Times* crossword puzzles; she would rattle off obscure words in answer to arcane clues with impressive confidence, always waving away admiration. Inevitably, these types of puzzles became too difficult for her, so I introduced her to word jumbles, which held her attention until her eyesight deteriorated too much to distinguish the small printed letters. But Grace has never tired of jigsaw puzzles; she will sit for hours at the dining room table, trying to piece her puzzles together. As the stages of Grace's disease progressed, the nature of the puzzles evolved—larger pieces, simpler patterns. After experimenting with different puzzles, I found one to be particularly engaging. It was a picture of a yellow lab that looked like our Sasha, who had been a great friend to Grace before passing away in 2008. Believing familiarity could be a good thing, I bought an identical puzzle so she could have one on the table in Palm Desert during the winter and one in Calgary during the summer. If I ask Grace if she wants to work on her puzzle, she will often demure, saying, "It's too hard." But if I suggest that we try to find two pieces that go together, she will sit down and begin to go through the pieces carefully, oblivious to me. Whenever she gets to the point of completion, it is easy to undo part or all the puzzle when she is not looking. With the memory of the completed puzzle already gone, she will resume working on the puzzle as if there had been no interruption.

For Grace, even in this late stage of her disease, the puzzle is still a permanent fixture on the table. Though the puzzle is constant, her dexterity at arranging the pieces has declined steadily, a clear marker of the progression of the Alzheimer's disease. At the outset, she could complete the entire puzzle by herself. Later, she could connect the edge pieces to frame the puzzle, but she needed help to complete the center of the puzzle. Now, we only undo four or five pieces for her, and then let her complete the puzzle. Her eyesight is almost totally gone, which has nothing to do with her Alzheimer's disease, but it has made things more difficult for her. She doesn't complain about her eyesight, but she can't differentiate the colors of the puzzle pieces and instead uses her fingers to feel where a piece is missing. She progresses through each piece, feeling them and manipulating them experimentally to fill a void in the puzzle. Her two impairments—Alzheimer's disease and blindness—blend together so that it is hard to distinguish the dominant villain. Though the near blindness seems the lead culprit, it is clear that Grace struggles to remember. Now, she will often force a lobe into a cove even when they do not fit together or place the puzzle pieces on the table with the wrong side facing up. Recently, while I was watching her work on her puzzle, I saw her working a particular space, trying unsuccessfully to make the piece fit. She could feel that there was one lobe that simply had no place to go. And I was startled when I saw her suddenly tear the offending lobe off the puzzle piece and squeeze the remaining part triumphantly into the space. She still finds solutions even when they don't seem like solutions to me. I look sometimes at Grace's favorite puzzle, with its pieces misplaced and jammed together, and what I see is the jumbled network of her ravaged mind. My throat constricts to see how much she struggles to accomplish things that bring her happiness. It is a feeling that I know well.

Although I believed I could always find some strategy to manipulate the situation, I have long felt unsure about how much authority over Grace's life I should take. With medical decisions, I felt comfortable, but with all the other aspects of structuring her life and her decisions, I was cautious. Taking responsibility for Grace's life meant admitting that my best friend was no longer able to make her own life decisions. I was grieving her loss every time my power in her life grew. Over time and with practice, a revelation dawned on me slowly: as her caregiver, I was responsible for her medical care as well as for managing every other part of her life. It weighed on me at first, but I soon realized that I was making arbitrary distinctions, seeing responsibility in some places but not others. Grace's health was not an aspect of her life; it was a product of her life. Everything that she did, everyone she spent time with, everything around her contributed in some way to her health. As her caregiver, I needed to accept that my role was pervasive. There were no neat lines demarcating the boundaries of my power. It was a terrifying insight at first. But the more I considered it, the more it seemed accurate.

Increasingly, caring for Grace made me intimately familiar with the aspects of her daily experience, and her community of friends and family became my responsibility as well. Her disease was a liability, and at all times, I needed to manage that liability in order to keep her safe. It took me a long time to accept the extent of my role in shaping Grace's life and the real consequences that always followed from my decisions. Recognizing that I was responsible for all aspects of Grace's life gave me strength in difficult situations, but it also increased the strain I felt in making decisions for her. Faced with a choice on Grace's behalf, I often thought about how much easier it would be if the decision was truly my own. But instead, I have been the person who put into motion the desires and decisions of the whole family, filtered through my own best judgment and intimacy with Grace.

Over the past decade, my ability to strategize has been tested time and again through the various stages of this disease. In many ways, I have approached my own life as a game of chess: I look for my path, I anticipate resistance and attacks, and I adapt as the game changes. Grace's illness initially felt like a surprise move by an opponent. After the diagnosis, however, I found myself sitting at an entirely new board, and it took me a long time to realize that I was now playing for Grace. And even now, I've never quite learned how to play Grace's chess game with the same confidence as I play my own. It is harder to see the path forward on Grace's board and harder to anticipate trouble. I always know how to define an acceptable loss for myself, but in my heart, no loss is acceptable for Grace, especially not on my account. I have lost so much of her already, and I know that I am now reliving the game I played during my first chess competition. There are not many pieces on Grace's board, and I am playing defensively to keep the game going. This time, however, I would be happy to call it a draw. I know the prospects. I know that defeat looms. And I know I will feel like it was my defeat because somehow, when it really counted, I could not come up with a strategy to save Grace.

***

I sit across from Grace, watching her as she rests in her favorite chair. She is at peace, which is all I ask for these days. Just after Christmas this year, there was a sudden and dramatic change in her condition. During these last few months, her ability to communicate has become more and more limited. She tries to make conversation by beginning a sentence that seems appropriate, but a few words into each sentence, she seems to lose focus and starts choosing her words at random. It is difficult to know if she realizes what is happening. Sometimes she seems quite agitated, shaking her wrist with the frustration of trying to find the right words. Other times, she seems not to notice or care. I try to interpret her meaning, but often her words are nonsensical. I find myself wondering whether it is as difficult for her to understand me as it is for me to understand her. She is good at pretending she understands others, but I have come to know that she uses her signature gay laugh to cover up for the fact that she has no idea what is being said. Although she seems to generally respond to directions, there are times, such as when I ask her to turn around so that I can help lower her into her chair, that she is entirely incapable of understanding me and I need to physically steer her around.

There are short periods of clarity, but clearly Grace has entered into a new, more difficult stage in this disease, and I am struggling to accept it. It seems so unfair that Grace has to endure this and that those of us around her have to witness it. I feel it weighing on me, and I can see that it weighs on Peter as well. Sharing a home with Grace lets us be close to her, but increasingly, it means that we are close to her Alzheimer's disease, and sometimes one overshadows the other. Peter used to enjoy sitting with Grace, being close to her and answering her endless loop of "How are the girls? Tell me about Chelsea, Lindsey, and Katie." Now, he is clearly uncomfortable being with her. When I ask him about it, I can see how close his emotions are to the surface. He chokes as he explains that seeing his mother like this, so confused and confusing, is painful, and I understand him exactly. It is hard to feel connected to Grace now that our lines of communication are almost totally cut off, and there is a hopelessness that we both feel but don't like to admit. This disease is so unkind.

When I reflect back over the last ten years, it is easy to see how significantly Grace Alzheimer's disease has shaped our lives. Throughout each stage of the disease, there have been challenges and difficulties, but also surprises and laughter. Although Alzheimer's disease is heartbreaking, I have never lost sight of the person that Grace is even as she changes right in front of me. I am grateful for everything that we have shared along the way. She is witty, intelligent, and giving. Grace, through her disease, has caused me to be a better person. She has taught me a patience I never knew existed and an unconditional love I will cherish forever.

The Grace that I know and love is increasingly isolated behind a wall that won't let us converse very easily. But every now and then a message is slid through the cracks in that wall. I have learned to slow down when I am with Grace and to appreciate the moments when she reaches out for me. Most nights, once Grace is settled in bed, I lie down beside her and put my arms around her. Words have begun to fail us, but being close to her sets us both at ease. Last night while I was holding her, I heard her say softly, "We get along well, don't we?" and I felt tears spring into my eyes as I kissed her cheek in agreement. Whatever stages remain, I know that she and I will face them together. Because, as Grace says, we get along well.

Edwards Brothers Malloy
Oxnard, CA USA
October 17, 2014